Wild Edens

NUMBER TWENTY-SEVEN:
The Louise Lindsey Merrick Natural Environment Series

Wild Edens

AFRICA'S PREMIER GAME PARKS
AND THEIR WILDLIFE

Joseph James Shomon

TEXAS A&M UNIVERSITY PRESS
College Station

Library of Congress Cataloging-in-Publication Data

Shomon, Joseph James, 1914 –

Wild Edens : Africa's premier game parks and their wildlife /
Joseph James Shomon. — 1st ed.

p. cm. — (The Louise Lindsey Merrick natural environment
series ; no. 27)

Includes bibliographical references and index.

ISBN 0-89096-801-2

1. Wildlife refuges — Africa. 2. Endangered species — Africa.
I. Title. II. Series.

SK571.S48   1998

508.676 — dc21   97-53174

CIP

To my nephew,

Anthony P. Shomon,

and his wife,

Roberta Shomon

Contents

List of Illustrations   ix

Foreword   xi

Prologue: Why Africa?   xiii

CHAPTERS

1.   Under the Spell of Kilimanjaro   3

2.   Elephant Country: Amboseli, Tsavo, and Salt Lick   13

3.   The Aberdares and Mount Kenya: Fragments of the High Rain Forest   25

4.   Avian Wonder Lakes of the Great Rift Valley   35

5.   The Seething Plains of Serengeti and Masai Mara   43

6.   Olduvai, Manyara, and Ngorongoro: Singular Worlds Apart   55

7.   The Marvels of Samburu and Meru   65

8.   Approaching the Mountains of the Moon   79

9.   Desert and Delta: The Kalahari and Okavango   91

10.   Namibia: A Symphony in Sand and Rock   99

11.   South Africa: Its Wondrous Wilds and Refuges of Hope   109

Appendix 1.   David Livingstone and the Wilderness He Loved   121

Appendix 2.   National Parks, Game Preserves, and Wildlife Sanctuaries in East, Central, and Southern Africa   131

Appendix 3.   Guidelines for an African Safari   141

Index   145

Illustrations

1. Mount Kilimanjaro 4
2. David Livingstone and Henry M. Stanley 7
3. Salt Lick Lodge 16
4. Giant Tsavo bull 18
5. Author examines field of elephant jaws 20
6. Angered bull elephant 22
7. Entrance to the Ark 28
8. Giant forest hogs and buffalo 30
9. Solitary leopard 44
10. Lioness laps up water 46
11. Male lion 48
12. Burchell's zebra 50
13. Ngorongoro black rhino with calf 60
14. Common cheetah *(left)* in contrast to the rare king cheetah. 62
15. Endangered wild dog 71
16. Leopard on a monkey kill 74
17. White rhino 75
18. Murchison Falls 83
19. Nile perch 84
20. Waterfowl 85
21. Cheetah 87
22. Sparsely vegetated riverbed 100
23. Dry Naukluft Mountains 104
24. Adventuring in the Namib wilderness 105
25. Gang of hippos 111
26. Steenbok 112
27. Nyala antelope ram 115
28. Warthog 117
29. Young elephants 118
30. Zebras must drink every day 123

31.   Zebras flee from danger   124
32.   Wildebeest   125
33.   Dominant female hyena   126
34.   Ruins of the Sultan's palace   127
35.   Author and wife at the Livingstone-Stanley marker   129

COLOR SECTION ONE   *Following page* 48

Masai men dancing
Crossing the Athi River
Bougainvilleas
Climbing Mount Kenya
Defiant Cape buffalo
Wildebeest
Lake Manyara tree-climbing lion
Two cheetahs attacking
Female ostrich with young
Klipspringer
Victoria Falls
Crocodile on a sandbar
Ugandan boys on termite castle

COLOR SECTION TWO   *Following page* 80

Baobab tree
Gannet rookery
Zebra and chimpanzees at Jane Goodall's camp
Maun women in colorful costumes
Hyenas feeding on a dead elephant
Waterberg Park for Endangered Species
Cape fur seal rookery
Welwitchia
Giraffe and zebra
View of canyon from atop Lesotho
Rock hyrax
Jackass penguins
Cape of Good Hope

Foreword

I first met Dr. Shomon when we were both working on advanced degrees at the University of Michigan. This was in the fall of 1956. A group of us met regularly for Sunday morning breakfast, with the topic of discussion usually revolving around conservation. One of our group was Whit Floyd, state forester of Utah, on special leave for two college semesters to do extra work. Whit and I were thoroughly indoctrinated about Africa by our colleague Joseph Shomon, especially as regards its parks and endangered wildlife. However, it was not until I retired from the California Department of Forestry in 1978 that I was able to respond to Dr. Shomon's many invitations to accompany him on a trip to East Africa. He set up a wonderful itinerary in Kenya, including visits and stays at several safari camps. This proved to be an extraordinary adventure and never-to-be-forgotten experience. It fully enriched and balanced my sense of conservation ethics.

This book covering Africa's wild edens describes a natural resource that is unique in our time, a living legacy that, if lost, would be irreplaceable. This would be tragic for us all. It would mean that future generations would be robbed of a rich and fascinating inheritance.

While I deeply applaud current efforts to establish gene pools for endangered wildlife, such as are in progress in Texas, Arizona, California, and elsewhere, these measures should not be considered efforts of last resort. The main focus should be directed at safeguarding and conserving endangered wildlife in native surroundings. This means the elimination of poaching and other illegal methods of taking wildlife. It also calls for better management of parks and wild areas, with emphasis on habitat restoration and conservation. The task ahead is formidable. It is essentially one of developing the will and allocating the human resources to get the job done.

Dr. Shomon wrote this book to reveal the magnificence and mystique of the African scene and in the hope of arousing further support and interest among the reading public, especially travelers, photographers, scientists, researchers, and conservationists, so that Africa's wild edens, particularly its game parks and sanctuaries, will continue to serve humankind for generations to come.

Heyden P. Reinecker
M.S.F.
Sacramento, California

Prologue

WHY AFRICA?

Why read books about Africa or why go there? This part of the world possesses treasures no other place on earth can duplicate—an extraordinary legacy of the still primitive, still wild, still free, and all this on a wide scale. That legacy includes not only the big game, small game, bird life, and other fascinating life forms but also the opportunity of seeing and meeting the decent, unpretentious, friendly local people themselves.

But basically it is the tremendous assemblage of wildlife, the spectacle, that is the chief drawing card in Africa. Modern travelers find it hard to believe that one can still actually witness wildlife dramas that daily evoke epochs when large mammals ruled the world and we were but half-wild creatures grasping for a foothold on the evolutionary ladder. Although the staggering numbers of game that once roamed the plains and bushlands of Africa are gone, even the remnants are sufficient to awe and enthrall the visitor. Where else can one see forty thousand wildebeest, twenty thousand gazelles, fifteen thousand zebras, and a thousand giraffes, plus groups of elephant, buffalo, lion, and hyena, all in a single day's game drive on the plains? Is there any spot on earth outside the Great Rift Valley where a million flamingos can be seen resting or feeding on just one lake?

In these fast-changing times, besieged as we are by impersonal high technology, excessive mechanization, and far too much artificiality, it is difficult to judge just what kind of world of the future we are building or undoing. Add to this the plethora of bad news coming over the media each morning and evening, citing one international crisis after another, plus the perpetual reporting of violence, dishonesty, and discord—and social ills—on our domestic front, and you have a dismal portrait of our nation and its people. Under these circumstances, where does conserving the natural environment fit into the picture? Moreover, what is the relevance of such matters as endangered African wildlife in our stressful world?

There are those who feel our tenure on earth is brief and we must look to other planets for new life and a more habitable world. So billions upon billions of dollars are spent on planetary probes and space research, while at the same moment programs in education, environmental improvement, and the correction of serious social ills are being curtailed. To most conservation thinkers and environmentalists, our national and global priorities are out of line and should be reversed. What is the sense of trying to find possible life on Mars or Venus, at enormous effort and expense, and then shortchanging our efforts to preserve life on a planet we know to be good and one proven to be salubrious to life? Why allow some of our largest wild land mammals to disappear before our eyes, as is happening today in Africa, while we recklessly overspend on space gadgetry and nuclear weapons?

There appears to be a strong feeling on the part of most Americans that our government is far behind the wishes and views of prudent people, especially on the goals and priorities set before us. As with the breakup of the Soviet Union, the power of people in America is beginning to assert itself, and this may yet save us.

One of the tenets of conservation long recognized in the United States, but insufficiently practiced, is the belief that most people will protect and safeguard those things they appreciate and consider of value, be these natural assets or well-established principles of human conduct. However, appreciation arises from understanding and knowledge. Thus, for example, if we want to save the African elephant and rhino, we must fully understand what the stakes are and what must be done to achieve success. As a longtime forester–wildlife biologist and ecologist, I am deeply convinced that we can turn our priorities around and make our planet a better place for humankind and all other species of life that share the good earth with us. It will take great effort and real commitment but it can be done. It must be done—and soon—otherwise our future looks bleak and may be short-lived.

Why should we place a high price tag on African wildlife? It is after all far away, in another world, and many of us will never get there to see it. But some of us today and those in future generations may indeed get there, and it would be consoling to think that they too would be able to experience the special power of the great game fields of Africa.

Today the idea of wildness or wilderness is beginning to be recognized as both a natural con-

dition and a state of mind. As the world continues to shrink, such priceless and irreplaceable conditions will assume greater and greater importance in our future. Wildness is in our genes and has been part of our ancestry since time immemorial. Our future is inherently tied to our knowledge and understanding of this trait. And nowhere is wildness more pronounced, more observable, than in wild Africa.

Another reason why the edens of the African wild are important to us and to the rest of the world is that their preservation is the rightful and morally correct thing for our human species to do. By taking a wise stewardship role in the preservation and conservation of this unique natural resource, we will be on the side of human goodness and right. Ownership of habitat and wildlife cannot be viewed in terms of possession, in the long run. Europeans and North Americans, having destroyed much of the wildness in the territory we do own, now owe it to the Africans, ourselves, and the human species as a whole to do whatever we can to prevent the remaining grand nodes of wildness from likewise disappearing.

A question arises about concern for African wildlife when millions of people are going hungry or starving to death. Could not the game be used to feed the impoverished people of Ethiopia, Sudan, Mali, Mozambique? It could. But this would be irresponsible, for soon the wildlife would be gone, eaten, and the starving masses would shortly be hungry again. The wiser, more prudent course would be to sustain the resource and use it wisely as a tourist attraction and thereby reap economic benefits for all of the people. This is what is being done effectively in Kenya, Tanzania, and several countries in southern Africa, notably Zimbabwe, Botswana, South Africa, and Namibia.

On the question of danger to travelers in Africa, let it be said that risk to tourists in East, Central, and southern Africa is small; it is unfortunate that the media have made much of the rare incidents of ambush in Africa. The average American, Canadian, or European is more prone to danger in the streets or on the highways at home than he or she would be on safari. While there are racial tensions in South Africa, these also continue to exist in Boston, Chicago, Detroit, New York, Washington, D.C., and London. Yet travelers continue to visit these cities. What's more, in South Africa and Namibia, safari travelers rarely see evidence of the troubles they have read about in the newspapers. One can put aside fears of injury while traveling the hinterlands of Africa for, statistically, the dangers are almost nil. As for attacks by animals themselves, this again has been terribly exaggerated. Attacks on humans by wild animals have occurred, of course, but if one obeys the rules and avoids reckless behavior, the chance of being gored by a buffalo, clawed by a lion, or trampled by an elephant are about zero.

Wild Africa today continues to enthrall the world with its wildlife—a vision made real because of the many game parks and wildlife preserves that have been established. The tourist trade is the number one industry in Kenya and is fast coming to the top in Tanzania. Elsewhere in Africa, too, wildlife, tourism, and a stable economy are inextricably linked together.

Finally, there is yet another reason to consider a trip to Africa: to answer a deep yearning to return to the bosom of Mother Earth—to the cradle of our ancestral beginnings. For it was here that our own species arose and commenced its ascent to human destiny.

Wild Edens

CHAPTER I

Under the Spell of Kilimanjaro

High above the plains of the southern Kenya wildlife sanctuary called Amboseli National Park, eye and mind suddenly confront an amazing spectacle. Silent, immutable, it seems to hover in space. In an equatorial land of shimmering heat waves and heavy ultraviolet light, one might momentarily wonder whether this unbelievably lovely sight is a mirage. Not so, however; the presence is the summit of a snowcapped mountain, its lower reaches shrouded in layers of dense fog and cloud. It is Kilimanjaro, the highest, boldest, most impressive peak on the continent and the undisputed mystical ruler of all East Africa.

To the repeat visitor no less than to the first-time beholder, the sight of this incredible mountain is immeasurably touching. One's heartbeat quickens. Especially when viewing the mountain at close range, some people are so mesmerized that they seem to stand like pillars of salt. Any physical or spiritual entity in nature that can do this to a human being must be credited with extraordinary powers. And Kilimanjaro has them. At 19,340 feet above sea level, this singular, all-pervading, freestanding equatorial massif radiates

more power than perhaps any other mountain on the face of the earth.

Physically, Kilimanjaro is a storehouse of geothermal energy, its pent-up dome continually emitting harmonic tremors that can be felt for miles around. Its interior furnaces steadily spew out plumes of fire and vapor. Volcanologists predict that, should Kilimanjaro someday blow its top, the eruption of Mount St. Helens would be dwarfed in comparison. Spiritually, the mountain is a supernatural being, holding all things in a kind of mysterious spell. Its enchanting force is part of what draws people to visit Africa.

One senses the power of Kilimanjaro even before actually landing at Tanzania's Kilimanjaro International Airport at Arusha or Kenya's Embakazzi International Airport at Nairobi. Seen from a jetliner arriving at dawn from Europe or America, the mountain may just be unfurling against the backdrop of an illuminating sun. Eager passengers who flock to the left portholes are rewarded with a never-to-be-forgotten visual and sensual experience.

In Kenya, the summit of Kilimanjaro can be

fig. 1. Mount Kilimanjaro rises out of the mist and bush of northern Tanzania.

seen from as far away as Nairobi, the nation's capital city. The snowy mantle can be seen from the upper floors of most hotels because the city is located on a mile-high plateau bordering the Great Rift Valley. The (now suburban) Ngong Hills made famous in Izak Dinesen's *Out of Africa* as well as the higher ground of Elspeth Huxley's *Flame Trees of Thika* also are good viewing sites. For closer viewing, Amboseli and its environs are excellent choices, with the added attraction of such big game animals as elephant, zebra, and giraffe often seen in the foreground. Usually the best time for viewing is in the clear atmosphere of early morning, when the mountain evokes an Egyptian camel bearing a load of white bed linens. Later in the day, viewing is apt to be disappointing as the great mountain often is concealed by clouds and rising fog. Visibility is said to be good for at least a hundred fifty days of the year. The less favorable viewing days usually occur in the rainy seasons (November and December and April, May, and early June). But Kilimanjaro is an elusive phenomenon and can show itself briefly at almost any time.

Aside from Amboseli and the eastern plains of Serengeti National Park (in Tanzania), perhaps the best viewing point for Kilimanjaro is a little-known site some eight miles east of Amboseli called the Hemingway Overlook. Here the famous writer and hunter Ernest Hemingway is said to have camped and perhaps even penned part of *The Snows of Kilimanjaro.* This overlook is a marvelous area, from which three major ecological zones on the mountain can clearly be seen: the wide, forested base; the more treeless midsection with prevailing arctic–alpine tundra conditions; and the four-thousand-foot icy and snowy summit itself. Those who have spent time studying, photographing, or painting the mountain consider the Hemingway Overlook the finest viewing site for Kilimanjaro in all East Africa.

If you spend enough time absorbing the mountain here, sooner or later the desire to climb it may become an irresistible urge. Some first-time visitors to Africa like to put the mountain climb first on their itinerary, thinking that reaching the top of Kilimanjaro will be an exciting introduction to the continent. It is not a bad idea, but one must be in good physical shape to do it. The mountain has roots in Tanzania and is only three degrees south of the equator. Many adventurers go to northern Tanzania (the best route) to make the climb, and an ever growing number of hikers actually reach the top. But even a partial climb can be a rewarding experience. In 1984 I led a party of ten up the mountain. While we did not reach even the Saddle at fourteen thousand feet, it was an episode for the memory book.

As imposing a geographic feature as it is, Mount Kilimanjaro was unknown to the western world until comparatively recently. Ludwig Krapf and Johannes Redmann, German missionaries, reported to outsiders the existence of Mount Kenya and Mount Kilimanjaro only in 1848–49.

And it was not until 1889 that a European climbed Kilimanjaro. Credit for this feat goes to geographer Hans Meyer and his alpine mountaineer partner, Ludwig Purtscheller, who made it to Kibo peak. Both were German.

The climbing of Kilimanjaro today is not a rare event. Hundreds of hikers do so each year. Those who reach the top report gaining a marvelous perspective of East Africa, and even for those who stop short, the experience is tremendously rewarding. No special skills are needed, but perseverence and good health are essential. Most climbers choose the traditional Tanzania route, starting from Kibo Lodge—a delightful hotel in the forested foothills—then riding a van to the entrance gate of Kilimanjaro National Park. Here permits are secured and arrangements made to rent or purchase sleeping bags, extra clothing, and food. The services of a guide and porters also are secured. Altogether, five days are needed for the complete mountain climb, three days going up and two coming down.

What is it like to climb Kilimanjaro? The event is not only a sobering exercise in climbing over snow but offers as well a firsthand lesson in tropical montane ecology. Several distinct life zones, each with characteristic flora and fauna, are crossed before reaching the snow line and tackling the snowy peak proper. Imagine dropping in on a party already well up the mountain. The group consists of six young to middle-aged hikers plus an African guide, four porters, and a cook. The hikers have their hearts set on making it to the roof of Africa. Already they have crossed the picturesque zone of juniper and *Podocarpus* trees and they now find themselves in the open grassy Saddle, which as noted is at about fourteen thousand feet. The wide plains below seem to stretch to infinity. Both mammals and birds appear scarce.

Loudly squeaking rock hyraxes, or dassies, scurry about among the volcanic boulders. The size of a rabbit but with a chunkier body and very short ears, the strange and unusual creature is more closely related to elephants and dugongs than to any other small mammal. High overhead two crowned eagles soar on the thermals. The Saddle is mostly covered with grass, heath plants, small rocks, and large boulders, many adorned with colorful lichens. Volcanic ash now is everywhere. Soon the group begins to tackle the great mantle of snow. At this higher elevation, roughly 14,500 feet, stops are frequent for the going gets more taxing, the air more rarified, and the cold starts to pinch the lungs.

At one rest stop the guide looks up and sees only massive dark clouds. The summit, he explains, is another four thousand feet upward. The prospect of the arduous trek ahead causes some hearts to sink. One climber wonders whether the reward will be worth the toil. Another is convinced that reaching the top would be a memorable achievement, a challenge met, a dream come true; moreover, if the skies should be clear, there would be a grand chance to see much of East Africa.

The group pushes on. Suddenly the last cloud layer is pierced and there, a thousand feet above, looms the crater's rim—the summit of Kibo. Adrenaline seethes through every climber. Now a supreme effort must be made to gain the top. But high-altitude nausea has overtaken two of the climbers. They decide to return to Top Hut, accompanied by a porter, to await the return of the others. It is an agonizing moment but a wise decision. An hour and a half later the advancing stalwarts reach Gilman's Point on Kibo peak.

Kilimanjaro is theirs! But the rejoicing is brief. With the temperature well below freezing, they can stay no more than twenty minutes. Luckily, the visibility is excellent. The climbers sign the register, jump up and down to keep the circulation moving, and look around.

The views are thrilling. Across the Tanzanian border in Kenya lies Nairobi, sprawled out on a green plateau along the south rim of the Great Rift Valley. The Rift Valley continues northward toward Ethiopia, Israel, Syria, Lebanon, and Turkey. Ahead are the rain-soaked Aberdare highlands and the twin icy peaks of Mount Kenya. On the eastern slope of Mount Kenya is Meru National Park with its winding Tana River. Here a small group of northern white rhinos is making a stand for survival.

To the east are the lowlands of the eastern and western sectors of Tsavo National Park and the Taita Hills, areas that are home to elephant, rhino, leopard, and bushbuck and where in the early 1900s man-eating lions prowled. The Kenyan port city of Mombasa lies beyond, its island harbor bathed gently by the tepid waters of the Indian Ocean. The island of Zanzibar, farther south, was the center of the abominable slave trade and ivory market in the eighteenth and nineteenth centuries. It was the port that gave East Africa so much dramatic history. Zanzibar also was where early explorers entered "darkest Africa." Here the names of Grant, Burton and Speke, Livingstone, and Stanley made history. Mombasa came to predominate as a shipping port because of the Mombasa-Uganda Railway, with spur lines extending into what were then called Tanganyika and Northern Rhodesia (now Tanzania and Zambia). Because Africa had so few suitable ports along its eastern coastline, Mombasa inevitably

fig. 2. David Livingstone and Henry M. Stanley.

was to play an increasingly important role in East Africa's development and trade.

Looking southward, a wide ribbon of savannah stretches all the way to Lake Malawi (formerly Lake Nyasa), including several national parks set aside to protect elephant, lion, buffalo, rhino, giraffe, wildebeest, and antelope populations. Finally, across the dim western horizon lies a land of volcanic mountains, valleys, granite hills, and great lakes. The immediate flatlands are the great plains of the Serengeti and the large lakes are Lakes Victoria, George, Albert, and Tanganyika. The Mountains of the Moon, an equatorial range with long lines of snow-covered peaks, lie beyond.

Clouds begin to form on Kibo, but the sister peak, Mwenzie, is still clear. The twenty-minute stay is up and the descent to Top Hut must be-

gin. The cold is so intense now that a brisk walk down the snow mantle is welcome. If no mishaps occur, the group will reach Top Hut by nightfall and in the morning will descend to Horombe Hut, followed later by a trek to the Saddle and on down to the base camp.

Soon the climbers are back at the Marangu huts at the main base of Kilimanjaro, exhausted but joyous. Everyone must stay a day to rest and get reacclimated to the lower elevation, just six thousand feet. Then the final hike down to the park gate will be easy. At Marangu there is time to reflect on the climbing experience and, perhaps, why some climbers have come to Africa. However, there is no need to dwell on these more sobering thoughts now for the impressions gained will remain with every climber for a long time.

Now it is still light enough for some relaxing reading while the cook is preparing a hot meal.

An ideal subject to be reading about after seeing the staggering vistas from atop Kilimanjaro is Africa's geography. Broadly, the great continent is a gigantic elevated plateau with bordering mountains and narrow coastal plains. Although desert and semidesert make up three-fifths of the continent, heavy rainfall occurs in some areas and is responsible for sizable tropical rain forests and great rivers, such as the Nile (the world's longest), the Congo, Niger, Zambezi, and others. Rainfall in the Mountains of the Moon is the highest in the world. In most parts of Africa the rains occur seasonally and there are long periods of no rain. And rainfall, of course, determines the character of the vegetation, which in turn determines the nature of the animal life.

In some ways there are really two Africas: low Africa and high Africa. The low consists of northern, western, and central areas with elevations from sea level to about two thousand feet. This region can be further subdivided into the coastal lowlands, northern highlands, Sahara plateau, western plateau, and the Nile and Congo basins. High Africa enjoys a cool, dry climate at elevations ranging from two thousand feet to more than nineteen thousand feet where Kibo peak soars to dizzying heights. This region has five subdivisions: the Rift system, eastern highlands, southern plateau, coastal plateau, and Madagascar (the fourth largest island in the world). Thus Africa has immensely varied landscapes and climate, which account for its rich and diversified fauna and flora and complex plant and animal ecology.

Staying in Kilimanjaro country a while offers an opportunity to learn something about the native people, the Masai and the Chagga, and

their sacred mountain. Legends are many. One is retold by an elderly Masai, known simply as Ben, who worked as a guard at Cottar's Camp on the Athi River in Kenya's Tsavo National Park. Ben liked to tell the saga of "The Fire Mountain."

It seems that once there lived in Africa a king called Menelik the First, who was said to be the son of King Solomon and the Queen of Sheba. After conquering all of East Africa, the king was on his way home one day accompanied by his entourage. At night while camping on the Saddle of Kilimanjaro, he had a strange premonition— that of death approaching. Something told the king to continue climbing, for at the summit of the great volcanic mountain a huge cauldron was boiling. Fires were burning fiercely under an immense vat. And it being very cold on the mountain, the thought of warmth was inviting. So the king summoned his advisors and a decision was reached: they would move upward. The group climbed up to the snowy crater of Kibo, next to icy Mwenzie, and somehow mysteriously vanished there, together with all the servants and the gold and jewels they wore and carried. But the legend has a happy ending. In short, at some point in the future some of King Menelik's offspring will arise and ascend Mount Kibo and discover and wear the great seal ring of the old king—and be imbued with the wisdom of King Solomon.

"And this, perhaps," old Ben always added, "wouldn't be so bad considering the state of affairs in the world today—Star Wars, Chernobyl, the fall of the Soviets and all that. Our overcomputerized world now is in bad shape. Do you not agree?"

Ben often offered to sing in Swahili to a "machine" (tape recorder) to entertain visiting groups. It was great, people said. But he always came back to the mountain. "It is alive," he would tell his audience. "It's full of fire . . . spirit. Twenty times I have felt the mountain shake. It is volcanic, you know, and can blow any time, like your Mount St. Helens." While the Masai remain in tune with the African wilds, they are not without modern communications.

The Masai are proud of their tradition as cattle herders. They roam the slopes of Kilimanjaro below ten thousand feet. Above that line is Kilimanjaro National Park, set aside as a scenic mountain reserve by the Tanzanian government some years ago. The Masai live in mud and dung dwellings called *manyattas* and subsist mainly on the milk and blood of their cattle. The manyattas are gradually being eliminated as the government is trying to encourage improvement over traditional living conditions. The Chagga are small farmers who cultivate tea, coffee, and banana plantations, live in small houses, and stay pretty much to themselves.

The call of wild Africa, like today's call of Kilimanjaro, was particularly strong during the past century and a half. Much of the continent south of the Sahara and north of a strip of development in southern Africa was virtually unexplored until 1850, little being known of East Africa and the interior. A thumbnail sketch of European discoveries begins with Portuguese mariners first sailing around the western and southern coasts in the fifteenth century. Vasco da Gama, the intrepid Portuguese navigator-explorer, rounded the Cape of Good Hope in 1498, then sailed up Africa's east coast, and finally crossed the Indian Ocean to India. Other explorers followed much later. The most significant were James Bruce, a Scot, who explored what is now Ethiopia, then traced the course of the Blue Nile to Khartoum, between 1770 and 1772. Hugh Clapperton, an En-

glishman, reconnoitered the central Sudan in 1821 and Richard Lander, also an Englishman, followed the Niger from Bussa to its outlet in 1830–31, proving that the river did not flow into the Nile or Congo, as many geographers had believed.

About this time, too, the English and Dutch began settlements in South Africa's Cape Province and missionaries started setting up their stations. Robert Moffat, a Scottish missionary, established a station at Kuruman, seven hundred miles north of Cape of Good Hope. More than a decade later, David Livingstone, who married Moffat's daughter, began exploring northward into Central Africa. After early forays into what are now Botswana, Namibia, and Angola, he later ventured into the regions of present-day Zimbabwe, Zambia, Mozambique, and southern Tanzania.

Sir Richard Burton and Captain John Speke, geographers, explored and argued over the Lake Victoria region in 1856–57. Livingstone came back to Africa in 1858 to help settle the controversy over the source of the Nile. He got bogged down on the lower Zambezi, necessitating the recall of his ill-fated expedition. He returned a third time, in 1866, became hopelessly lost in terrain now part of Zambia and western Tanzania, only to be miraculously found by Henry M. Stanley at Ujiji on the shores of Lake Tanganyika. The day was November 4, 1871.

Theodore Roosevelt, after his presidency, went to Africa on an extraordinary safari in 1909, principally to hunt and collect big game for the national museum in Washington, D.C. And Carl Akeley, famed American taxidermist, journeyed to East Africa five times (1896, 1905, 1909, 1921–22, and 1926) to secure trophy big game animals for a New York museum. He died of infection in the Ruwenzori Mountains in 1926.

Then came the fascinating era of Martin and Osa Johnson, famed American photographers and writers, who spent no fewer than sixteen exciting years in Africa—mostly East Africa—recording with black-and-white still pictures and movie film the vast animal herds of the African wilderness. No two people in recent times, certainly within the memory of many still living, did more to reveal to the world the true nature of Africa's stupendous wildlife than did this noted couple from the plains of Kansas. The Johnsons traveled on foot, by motor car, lorry, and airplane and obtained thousands of spectacular photographs and much movie footage of big game. They wrote best-selling books and produced two outstanding black-and-white talking motion pictures, *Baboona* and *Congorilla* (1930), which remain classics.

One especially fascinating adventure in Martin's life was his first flight over the great mountain of Kilimanjaro, also in 1930, in the company of his beloved pilot Vern Carstens and using Martin's amphibious plane named *Osa's Ark*. The noted photographer wrote that from his camp on Mount Kilimanjaro it was a magnificent sight when the clouds around the mountain's summit cleared away and gave them a view of its snow-covered crest. Often the great white arc of the summit seemed to them utterly cut off from the earth, floating like a mirage in the air. Finally, one perfect day, they decided to make a flight about the peak. They took off easily and climbed rapidly until they struck the clouds. Carstens at last brought the big ship above the clouds, and there, glistening in the vivid sunlight, the vast snow-covered crest lay before them, with the brown rocks below the snowfields somber and dark in contrast.

Today the lofty, bewitching Kilimanjaro continues to pour out its great spirit to all humankind, to all life. The call is not a blaring, self-seeking call for recognition, but rather a quiet, steadfast beckoning—an invitation for everyone to seek out the mountain's fascinating, wondrous legacy.

The call rings out not just from the snow-clad summit of Kibo but also from dozens of other wild edens in Africa—from the Aberdares, Mount Kenya, Tsavo, from the many Rift Valley lakes, from the Serengeti, Ngorongoro, and the Samburu and Meru bushveld—a tropical or subtropical forest of low trees and bushes. This call of the wild, in effect now also a distress call in places, comes from as far away as the Mountains of the Moon, the Virungas, the Zambezi valley, the Kalahari, and even from the haunts of many sanctuaries of hope in southern and southwestern Africa, including the very Cape of Good Hope—named in optimism, and optimism and positive approaches may now be needed more than ever—at the southernmost tip of the continent.

CHAPTER 2

Elephant Country

AMBOSELI, TSAVO, AND SALT LICK

Whether one has begun coming to grips with wild Africa by gazing upon and absorbing the force of Kilimanjaro or by hiking up it, the obvious next step is to travel across the lower bushveld into Kenya and get into the big game wilderness where the big five—elephant, rhino, lion, leopard, and buffalo—command attention. The focus of interest changes from striking mountain beauty and somewhat arcane flora and fauna to the lowland vegetation and wildlife, the classic great game herds of Africa. Most visitors to East Africa are not mountain climbers but want to see wild animals and are intent upon getting out of a city like Nairobi—the bustling capital city—and into the bush and under canvas as quickly as possible. Two nearby refuges, Amboseli National Park and Salt Lick Sanctuary (private), and the much larger Tsavo National Park are accessible and appealing places where one can be introduced to African wildlife right from the start of a visit.

AMBOSELI NATIONAL PARK was not always a popular place. True, it was for decades on the itineraries of tourists going to East Africa, but the interest was largely in the spectacular views of Mount Kilimanjaro rather than the occasional zebra or wildebeest. There were no real roads in Amboseli, only dirt tracks. More often than not, billowing dust covered the parched savannah, requiring tourists to wear goggles and face masks to protect themselves. Most people couldn't get away fast enough. But Amboseli has some remarkable springs and wetlands, including marshes and swamps, all filled with lush vegetation and many feeding elephants. Because of the lack of roads, these areas have been virtually off limits to vehicles.

Today Amboseli has hit the front pages of the world, although the habitats and species in the park have changed little. What has changed is our knowledge of the African elephant, its life history, behavior, and ecological relationships to other forms of life, including *Homo sapiens*. Credit for much of this must go to the research scientists who for several decades have been studying Amboseli elephants.

When the elephant population went into a serious decline after World War II, many scientists and researchers saw the need for more information on the tusker behemoth. First priority was to find a site where poaching could be eliminated and a sizable population of elephants could be studied without outside molestation. Amboseli won out as the perfect site. A long-range study project had to be planned, set up, funded, and staffed. Ecologist Dr. David Western helped initiate the project and the research work began. Scientists like Cynthia Moss, Joyce Pool, and others joined the effort, funded in part by the World Wildlife Fund, African Wildlife Foundation, and others. After several decades of intensive fact finding, the world now knows much more about elephants, information one hopes will become the basis for better future elephant management in Amboseli and elsewhere.

The African elephant *(Loxodonta africana)* is truly an imposing creature, the largest land mammal on earth. A big adult male can weigh up to six or seven tons and stand 11 feet or taller at the shoulder. It can drink up to forty gallons of water and consume 350 to 400 pounds of grass and browse daily, including tree branches and tree trunk fibers. To keep its huge body functioning, the elephant must feed a good part of the day and even at night. It does, however, take time out for traveling, resting, bathing, dusting, and playing. In these activities the elephant has been found to possess many attributes we tend to think of as human, such as joy, love, anger, loyalty, concern, grief, and even rivalry among siblings.

Elephants also display great intelligence; they remember events a long time and exhibit considerable patience and ingenuity. Little wonder that elephants have endeared themselves so much to people. The Asian elephant, a separate species, is a third smaller than the African, has smaller ears, and is the one most often seen in zoos and circuses. In India and other parts of Asia elephants are closely involved with human society and economy, having been trained to work in forestry.

In the late 1990s Amboseli had just short of seven hundred elephants, closely observed and monitored almost daily by research scientists. Much of what is now known about elephants and elephant society is due to the work of Cynthia Moss, an American biologist who worked out a system of identifying individuals by the vein patterns in their ears. Once an animal was positively identified, it could be named and its activities could be followed month by month, year by year. As a result, voluminous information has been compiled on elephant social arrangements, along with how family groups behave and live.

According to Cynthia Moss, a typical elephant family consists of ten or more individuals, mostly females (males leave the group after attaining sexual maturity, usually between the ages of ten and fifteen). Mature males join the family group for brief periods only during breeding time. There is some pushing and shoving among the bulls during this period, but seldom any serious fighting. A cow elephant in her prime, usually between fifteen and forty-five years of age, will mate and bring forth a calf every four or five years, the period of gestation being twenty-two months. A newborn calf may weigh 260 pounds and be 3 feet tall. It can stand almost immediately, begins to suckle promptly, and depends on its mother and other family members for protection, often for years.

One interesting and revealing guideline one can draw from the Amboseli observations is this:

When you see an elephant group that includes calves and other small elephants as well as larger adults, the chances are good that this is a family group. It will be dominated by an experienced old matriarch who calls the shots, giving all the signals for moving, traveling, stopping, feeding, bathing, playing. Groups of mature-looking elephants are probably bachelors keeping company together, some eventually breaking away to mate. Big tusker males are generally loners and, of course, are the ones most sought after by poachers.

SALT LICK SANCTUARY is one of the better places to see elephants and other big game. Here one can see Cape buffalo, rhino, zebra, giraffe, kudu, and warthog. The sanctuary is located in the Taita Hills, a two-hour minibus run from Amboseli. The habitat is primarily bushveld with sufficient clearings to make visibility quite good. This is a private sanctuary where no effort was spared in developing a perfect site for animal watching. One is struck by the attractive setting and by the clever and unusual design of the lookout facility. The visitor enters a concrete structure from behind, climbs one story, and then moves through spacious halls to several balconies. The natural stage below is a clearing with a water hole plus some scattered water pockets containing blocks of salt. The terrain slopes gradually upward so that several acres of habitat can be seen from one point. A few trees and clumps of vegetation are scattered about. An atmosphere of silence permeates the area and onlookers converse in whispers.

Almost always, some animals can be seen standing in the clearing, or approaching it, or drinking at the water hole. One is merely an inconspicuous observer looking in on the lives of animals in the wild. At night the area is bathed with artificial moonlight, producing an eerie setting.

The parade of game at Salt Lick is steady: small groups of impala and zebra moving about, several Cape buffalo grazing, giraffe munching among treetops, baboons suddenly testing the water, warthogs drinking, and groups of elephants numbering ten or twenty or thirty in the background, fanning their huge ears. Then more giraffe heads show up far in the back, all simply looking and looking, only to start slowly feeding with their long tongues on the topmost acacia limbs. The giraffe are a good 150 yards away but binoculars pick them up clearly. Now a family of ten elephants with a calf comes down the slope to the water hole and all begin to siphon water with their trunks. A family of warthogs comes into view and they too begin to drink. Three giraffes edge slowly down the slope, moving cautiously because experience has taught them that lions may be waiting in ambush. Reaching the narrow, fifty-foot-long water hole, they laboriously spread their front legs wider and wider until their long necks can finally lower their heads to the water surface; nervously, they commence to drink. The only sound is an occasional squeal from a baby elephant as its guarding mother nudges the infant to move along. When dinnertime comes for the human guests, small groups begin to move, by ones and twos, slowly toward the spacious and lovely dining room, where many tables overlook the great stage below.

Salt Lick Sanctuary has two buildings. One is a five-story hotel where visitors first arrive after traveling from Nairobi or Amboseli and rest up briefly and have lunch. It is Salt Lick's sophisticated transfer point before groups board a special

fig. 3. Salt Lick Lodge in the Taita Hills on the edge of Tsavo National Park.

bus late in the afternoon for the main observation structure five miles away. The sleeping accommodations and meals at Salt Lick are excellent.

In addition to its several observation decks, Salt Lick also offers a special underground tunnel leading to a pillbox where photographers and others can watch the parade of game from close at hand, in complete safety, without being noticed.

TSAVO NATIONAL PARK. If Amboseli has come into its own as a research setting, and Salt Lick has brought new sophistication to wildlife viewing, Tsavo is distinguished for its large size,

enabling this park to accommodate (and illuminate) ecological processes in a way that smaller reserves can never do. Tsavo, both West and East, comprises a huge national park with many habitats and numerous species of mammals, birds, reptiles, and fishes. The area is essentially a wilderness park with limited dirt roads and few accommodations. Safari groups usually stay two or three days, stopping at Mzima Springs, Safari River Lodge on the Athi River, or a bush lodge called Kilagoni. The park is so vast that a brief visit does not do it justice, although brief exposure is better than nothing.

Mzima Springs is one of the most underrated places in Tsavo West. Here a series of clear freshwater springs attracts elephants, buffalo, zebra, and giraffe plus a host of antelope, baboons and vervet monkeys, and warthogs. Waterbirds, like coots and ducks, arrive in great number, eyed by calling fish eagles and silent, solitary, statuesque herons, such as the goliath and others. Six species of kingfishers also come to feed here, as well as great flocks of sand grouse and many songbirds and insectivorous birds.

The secret to the drawing power of this oasis is the nutrients dumped into the water by the hippos—some ten tons of dung and urea every twenty-four hours. This creates a rich, nutritious soup for the production of microscopic plants and animals, which in turn sustain the larger animal forms, such as insects, fish, amphibians, and reptiles. These in turn become food for birds and mammals. In other words, Mzima is a microcosm of plant and animal life, a small but fabulous wonderland operating in the larger ecosystem that is Tsavo.

The spring water comes from the Taita Hills some twenty miles away, in the foothills of Kilimanjaro. When the rains fall in the volcanic hills, water seeps down through porous black basaltic rock until it strikes an impervious ledge. Then it flows down along a rocky incline to Mzima, to surface in a river-sized stream and a series of sparkling, jewel-like water holes. The pools contain some seventy hippos and numerous crocodiles and tilapia fish. There are walks and an underwater glass tunnel, from which visitors can see hippos, crocs, and fish swimming in their native habitat.

Tsavo as a whole constitutes the largest game park area in Kenya and one of the largest in Af-rica, covering an area of 8,034 square miles—about the size of the state of Massachusetts. The park extends over a vast expanse of semiarid bush country, stretching from the Tana River in the north to the Tanzania border in the south. On clear days the great mass of Kilimanjaro can be seen rising out of the highlands.

Authorities once estimated that the two sectors of Tsavo were home to some fifty thousand elephants that roamed in and out of the park, of which twenty thousand could be in the park at any one time. The park also once harbored most of Kenya's black rhinos, with a one-time estimated population of two thousand. Today, however, both are sadly diminished, the abominable work of poachers. While the elephant and rhino continue to be the park's two most charismatic species of big game, surveys (though difficult to make in this bushveld) have shown the presence of lion, leopard, cheetah, large herds of Cape buffalo, many giraffe, numerous zebra, wildebeest, and a wide variety of antelope, including impala and dik-dik.

Tsavo is noted for periodic drought and resulting fluctuations in the large mammal populations. Much of Tsavo East is flat country with acacia trees, baobabs, and thorny scrub, plus patches of open grassland. There are many areas of exposed sandy red soil, some caused in part by fires and some by tree felling by elephants. The whole western section of the refuge is broken by the Yatta Plateau, which used to have high populations of both elephant and rhino along the Athi and Tiva Rivers. Not so today. Poachers have killed off many of them.

The muddy Athi and Tiva Rivers in Tsavo East flow through a great wide valley. And while it is almost impossible to get through this bushveld

fig. 4. A giant Tsavo bull with broken tusks almost collides with our minibus.

by four-wheel-drive Land Rover, occasionally some adventurous diehards have done so and reported seeing incredible herds of elephants and buffalo. The animals apparently sweep across the bush between the rivers in their daily search for food and water, creating deep spoor trails. Elephants, in particular, move about in single file, often in herds of up to fifty. Mostly they are led by a big matriarch with other dominant females as a rearguard and the young zealously guarded somewhere in the middle.

Scientists and game wardens checking game by helicopter or trying to nab poachers have reported seeing as many as one hundred elephants in one migratory group. Seventy-five years ago, however, large herds in this area and in the Lake Paradise region of northeast Kenya (now Marsabit National Park) numbered into the thousands. Martin and Osa Johnson reported seeing as many as two thousand elephants together and photographed enormous herds. But today the long migratory pathways of elephants have been broken up, forcing the animals into smaller and smaller confines. Large as Tsavo is, it is still a confined area. In earlier times when drought struck, the big beasts could push out into new habitats, often hundreds of miles away. Not so now. No sanctuary is large enough to permit this kind of uninterrupted travel by large elephant herds.

When Tsavo became a national park and protective status was given all big game, the elephant herds as well as rhinos began to build up. By the end of 1969 the elephant population was bursting at the seams. No one knew how many elephants there were—perhaps thirty-five thousand, perhaps even forty-five thousand. Then in 1970 the rains failed. Many water holes dried up, and

the lesser rivers no longer held water. All during the winter and spring of 1970–71 the drought grew worse. Elephants and rhinos began losing weight. In desperation the tuskers tore down whole areas of forest, trying to get at the moisture and fibers of living trees, especially baobabs. In places vast woodlands were converted to grassland, with only skeleton trees remaining. Female elephants could no longer breed. Hundreds of pregnant cows, their ribs showing and their bodies terribly weakened by thirst and hunger, fell in their tracks. The concerned younger animals tried desperately to get them up, probing, trying to lift them up with their tusks, only to see the helpless die at their feet. Daylight scenes were nightmares; night sounds were those of a black hell.

The same thing happened to the elephant calves. Mothers would hover over them trying to get them up, only to fall to the ground themselves beside their young, panting, heaving, trumpeting up an eerie dirge of convulsive death. Some scenes in the backveld, as reported by the wardens, were even more appalling. Whole family groups stuck together but in the end went down to ignominious death, as if in a massive suicide pact. In other situations emaciated bulls went berserk, plowing through acacia groves in crazed abandonment, only to shriek, falter, drop, and expire in a series of agonizing death throes.

When at last in the winter of 1971 the work of the drought had done its worst, thousands upon thousands of elephants had died, along with at least six hundred rhino, their great carcasses strewn over much of the Tsavo landscape. Rangers and game guards collected elephant lower jaws and lined them up in neat rows so that biologists could study the teeth. The skulls were too big, too heavy to collect, so the tusks were removed and

fig. 5. The author examines a field of elephant jaws collected following the severe 1970 drought in Tsavo National Park, Kenya.

brought to a central collecting point. So vast was the assemblage of elephant lower jaws that it covered several acres—a grim sight to behold. Somewhere between eight thousand and ten thousand elephants perished in that devastating drought—an experience that will never leave the memory of any who witnessed it.

Could anything have been done to save the elephants? Efforts were made. Trees were cut down for food, wells dug, and water brought in. But elephants need huge amounts of water and food every day to survive. When prolonged thirst and starvation strike a large population of huge wild animals, people can do little. Only rains bringing enough food and water could have saved them.

The enormous tragedy of the Tsavo elephants made news around the world. The best of wildlife scientists were brought in to assess the problem and seek solutions. But no easy answers were found. The main lesson learned here was that all wild animals are limited by their food and water supplies—by the carrying capacity of the land. When populations exceed these restrictions they must be reduced to what the habitat will support;

nature will take its course. The question arises: Should people intervene in these circumstances and, if so, by what means and under what circumstances? In Tsavo legalized hunting by sportsmen was proposed. Another idea was the shooting of "surplus" animals by park officials or contractors for meat, hides, and ivory—also an unattractive solution. The scheme of trapping and removal was tried in a limited way, but how many five-ton elephants can anybody trap and safely remove from a big wild area with poor roads? Moreover, where can the money be found to meet such a costly undertaking?

There have been those who view the great Tsavo die-off as an example of the process of habitat alteration by a species—elephants in this case. Whereas the effects of the crisis were indeed sad and dismaying, and the park afterward looked so very different, even ravaged, the argument nevertheless was made for letting events take their course and letting a new kind of "equilibrium" take over—and subjecting that natural process to scientific scrutiny. Such thinking has advanced somewhat the impossibility of "static" conservation, the fact that all one can conserve may be processes. Thus such a large park presents incredible scientific opportunities, in contrast with smaller reserves where watching wildlife is at the fore, as at Salt Lick, or where intensive studies are easier to pursue, as at Amboseli.

The search for wise management goes on. One thing seems certain: the world needs to know a lot more about elephants in the wild, about different habitats, the extent of the food supply, and the amount of biomass present (tonnage of living animal matter in an area), before wise management can be put into practice. Answers can

come only from competent, long-range research. Fortunately, today, research in some areas is getting under way.

The elephants of Tsavo today are also under another threat: poaching. The killers are lawless individuals who use not only firearms but also death pits, poisoned arrows, cables, wire snares, even poisoned water to do their despicable work. During the past century poachers, supplying the reprehensible demand for ivory, have been responsible for the demise of hundreds of thousands, perhaps even millions, of elephants in Africa. Wholesale destruction of tuskers for ivory is one of the most unsavory sagas of brutalized killing ever to strike the animal kingdom.

Ivory has long been an item of trade and commerce, dating back to ancient times. The product comes chiefly from the hard tusks of elephants (and to a small degree from the walrus). Although Asian elephants have been part of the ivory trade, their numbers are small and the tusks are smaller in size than are those of the African elephant. Ivory is called "white gold" in Africa. While the trade in African ivory has been outlawed in most African countries, the "ivory war" is still being fought. As long as the value of this special material continues to climb in the world market, the African elephant's fate will remain in doubt. Its rapid decline is clearly evident all over Africa, but particularly in East Africa.

As destructive as poaching may be to African elephants, and as offensive as the practice is to all lovers of wildlife, the facts now show that elephants suffer from an even more basic threat: the destruction and despoliation of their essential habitat. The behemoths are continually being crowded into smaller and smaller areas, putting

fig. 6. An angered bull elephant about to charge.

ever greater pressure on the existing vegetation where elephants live. And because their former migratory routes have been cut off, distant foraging habitats are no longer available to them. As a result, hungry elephants frequently invade farmland and villages where they are often gunned down.

One estimate—according to a report by Wildlife Conservation International—reveals that over a million elephants roamed the savannahs and forests of Africa as recently as the 1980s. Now they are listed as a threatened species. Each year their numbers decrease. In some regions only remnant herds persist. In others, elephants are already but

a memory. Kenya, for example, has lost more than half its elephant population since 1972. And Kenya is one of the more advanced and stable countries in East Africa.

In Tsavo National Park, East and West, the elephants still have a chance. Better antipoaching techniques are being developed and more private money from the outside world is coming in for more personnel and equipment for the rangers who risk life and limb to catch the poachers. More than a hundred poachers were killed in Kenya after President Mao issued a "shoot to kill" order.

There is a bright spot in Tsavo. Recently a

25,000-acre special preserve was established to try to increase the numbers of the rhino. The area is fenced to keep the rhino in while other game can move in and out. With tighter patrolling in this limited area the future holds out promise.

Today, we see, unmistakably, that the world's largest land creature and humans are inextricably bound together. In the predicament of the African elephant we are beginning to see something of ourselves.

CHAPTER 3

The Aberdares and Mount Kenya

FRAGMENTS OF THE HIGH RAIN FOREST

Not so long ago, during the late 1960s and early 1970s, world attention suddenly focused on deteriorating tropical rain forest ecosystems. Not only was this vital living system disappearing but in many places around the globe it had already vanished, along with untold species of plant and animal life it supported. The principal causes were two: massive clear-cut logging operations by international timber corporations seeking vast profits and native forest people's traditional slash-and-burn-and-move-on land practices, which became a problem only because the increased population meant more people slashing and burning.

What triggered world outrage was not merely the operations themselves but the ecological effect this was beginning to have on global climatic conditions, earth warming, and the extermination of plant and animal life in the most prolific, most abundant system of life on earth. The most threatened areas include Central and South America; India, Indonesia, and Malaysia; and Africa. While conservation actions, efforts toward sustainable

use, and reforestation in some places have been launched to inhibit further destruction, much devastation continues. Today species loss is estimated by some at about seventy-five thousand each year, some of fauna and flora not yet even identified. In Africa the loss of forests and life forms has been most pronounced in the great Congo basin, where high rainfall lowlands produce heavy tropical growth. In East Africa, particularly in the drier highlands, there are virtually no rain forests left. However, the upper slopes of the Aberdare Range and Mount Kenya still display high altitude collars of true tropical rain forest. They are wondrous places to visit, and their life forms, particularly the big game, are worth some effort to see.

To many people the term *rain forest* conjures up strange jungle scenes of lush and impenetrable lowland forests, with giant poisonous snakes poised in the heavy greenery of huge trees or hanging liana vines, waiting to devour anything that moves. This of course is mostly a myth. But luxuriant vegetation does characterize tropical rain forests, especially lowland virgin forests, where plant and animal life is abundant and diverse in species. Sadly, such forests are disappearing in Africa and all around the world, a situation causing great concern for life on our planet. Today there are no lowland rain forests to speak of in East Africa, which is unfortunate. Because East Africa is largely an elevated, dry plateau, there is insufficient year-round rainfall to support the type of heavy growth typical of lowland tropical rain forests. But there are still some high altitude rain forests, and the Aberdares, Mount Kenya, Mount Kilimanjaro, and Mount Elgon are shrunken examples of such edens. Up in the mountains there is considerable year-round rainfall, so special zones of montane rain forest do occur. These lofty fragments and their wildlife are, in a sense, only microcosms of a once vast flourishing tropical rain forest, remnants of a once much larger forest ecosystem in East and Central Africa.

The most practical starting point for the Aberdares and Mount Kenya is Nairobi, close to two hundred miles away. In Kenya, open roof hatches on minibuses are permitted. On leaving Nairobi, one rolls slightly upward through the picturesque Ngong Hills and on past the famous estate of *The Flame Trees of Thika* with its spectacular blooming royal poincianas. The highway winds along the eastern escarpment of the Great Rift Valley, which drops away a dramatic two thousand feet below. Reaching into the clouds some one hundred miles away, and from far off looming deceptively as just more high country, the Aberdares support a rain forest range sixty miles long by thirty to fourty miles wide.

To break up the drive to the mountains, most people stop at Thompson's Falls. At this midway point one has an opportunity to stretch and photograph a lovely waterfall plunging into a deep chasm. It was named after Joseph Thompson, an English explorer who reconnoitered much of the region, including the Aberdare Mountains.

The same Joseph Thompson named the mountain escarpment the Aberdare Range in 1883. It may be good to remember at this point that only the upper reaches of the Aberdares and Mount Kenya have been set aside as national parks.

ABERDARE NATIONAL PARK is a 330-square-mile rain forest sanctuary, limited in size and yet a refuge of unheralded wonder and beauty. The area is little known beyond what can be seen from its two famous tourist lodges, Treetops and the Ark.

In the center of the Aberdares rises the 13,104-foot volcanic crest Lesatima, seldom seen because of frequent cloud cover. The topmost heights rise up from heavy rain forest and large stands of bamboo. All abound with mountain wildlife. Largely undeveloped except for a few dirt tracks and foot trails, the park surprisingly receives thousands of visitors each year, mostly due to the full bookings at the two lodges. And because the lodging is limited and tightly controlled, one sees few people other than those at the established facilities. Lodge visitors are held as happy prisoners in man-made facilities while the animals outside roam freely, a popular principle of management followed successfully for decades.

Treetops first opened many years ago but became famous in 1952 when Princess Elizabeth went up into the lodge as heir to the British throne and came down as Queen of England following the death of her father, King George VI. The lodge burned down once, was rebuilt, and has been scheduled for further improvement, even expansion. The viewing verandas overlook a floodlit clearing with a water hole and a muddy area with pockets containing blocks of salt. Here sightings of elephant, buffalo, rhino, bushbuck, giant forest hog, and baboon are common. Sometimes at night under artificial moonlight the rare bongo is sighted. And on few occasions, lion, leopard, and the common spotted hyena show up. Frequently genets and mongooses come around at night.

At both Treetops and the Ark, eight miles away, the power plants have been cleverly placed underground so that quiet prevails, especially important at night. It is customary to talk in a whisper, this applying both to the inside sitting areas and to the viewing balconies. The hushed atmosphere helps make the Aberdare mountain rain forest a unique experience.

Visitors to the highland lodges find the atmosphere cool, relaxing, refreshing, and surprisingly casually regulated. The key to successful management here has been and continues to be the so-called transfer stations in the foothills of the Aberdares. At each station the visitor registers, obtains a room key, and has a leisurely lunch. Extra luggage is stored at this point, for only one small bag per person can be taken to the lodge. Rooms at the Ark are small, each with two bunks. Showers and lavatories are down the hall.

At the Aberdare Country Club transfer point (for those going to the Ark), the spacious grounds overlook a vast expanse of green. Mount Kenya bristles in the distance. The transfer station for Treetops is called Outspan, and the procedure there is the same. Travel to the lodges is by special buses—a rough ride of about forty minutes. At Treetops the quarters are even more limited in space than at the Ark.

There is ample time to stroll around the beautifully kept hillside grounds. Colorful bougainvilleas always seem to be in bloom around both clubs. At Outspan, usually in December, the lovely lawns and golf course become a spectacle as thousands of fallen jacaranda tree flowers carpet the ground in a breathtaking sheen of lavender beauty.

The Aberdare Country Club has a fascinating walk-through aviary for bird lovers and photographers, a screened structure containing many different African birds in separate enclosures. Outside, one can also see and often approach wild African sacred ibis as well as stately crested and crowned cranes.

For those not booked at a lodge, traveling by car, and camping on their own, a dirt road winds up through the Aberdares to ten thousand feet, where the views of Mount Kenya become ever more impressive. The trees are festooned with old man's beard, a greenish drooping moss of exquisite beauty. The dirt track traces the spine of the Aberdares for several miles and at one point passes a foot trail leading to Chania Falls. The short trail, marked by a sign warning of lions, brings the visitor to a cataract dropping a thousand feet down into the lush, heavy forest below. Close by are the equally impressive Guru and Kururu falls, which send plumes of sparkling water cascading down the dark cliffs. It is little-known wild country that is well worth seeing.

One of the compensations of camping out is the fact that one may see and at night hear more wildlife. Besides spotting elephant, buffalo, giraffe, and giant forest hog, one may hear lion, leopard, and hyena. The Aberdares are also home to the now quite rare colobus monkey, a large black and white primate with long body fur and an extra

fig. 7. *Entrance to the Ark in Aberdare National Park, Kenya.*

long, white-haired tail. The more common mon-key, however, is the Abyssinian, which is black with some white on the face and flank. A secre-tive animal, the colobus favors tall trees with heavy cover where it can hide easily, perhaps a trait learned relatively recently when it was heavily hunted for its coat and tail. There is a reliable report that in 1892 as many as 175,000 colobus skins were exported to Europe alone. The skins were also prized in the Middle East, where specu-lation was that tears in the pelts were caused by the animals themselves when trying to avoid cap-ture. Now that international traffic in endangered species is coming under more controls, the colo-bus, which is distributed over a wide range in dense equatorial Africa, may be induced to return.

Tour groups scheduled for Treetops are met at the Aberdare National Park gate by an escort with a rifle for protection of the guests: the distance one walks to the lodge is only some 200 yards, but that can be enough for trouble to arise. One party encountered an agitated elephant bull, which had to be dropped in his tracks just ten feet away.

At the Ark the visitors step off their bus and promptly enter a protective four-hundred-yard el-evated walkway leading to the fabulous shiplike structure. Once inside, guests are shut in for the rest of the afternoon and night—an ordeal most "prisoners" accept with quiet delight because this retreat offers a quality experience in wildlife viewing.

At both watchtowers one is certain to see a variety of big game. The lodges are both sited at natural water holes. During the day game animals and waterbirds can be seen. The birds include a few ducks, coots, and herons. And seemingly ever present are marsh birds of the noisy rail family. At night mainly big game animals show up. A buzzer sounds when a particularly notable species appears. Viewing is from closed and open balconies or, at the Ark, also from a ground-level concrete pillbox connected to the lodge by a tunnel.

Most of the time some elephants will march in at night, usually in single file, eager to reach the rock salt placed on the ground. Here the behemoths stand and sip the saline ooze for long periods. On rarer occasions a lone black rhino may put in an appearance, an event that triggers the buzzer twice, sending photographers and others scurrying to their preselected observation posts.

Those who spend enough time at one of the lodges or who choose to go camping in the higher Aberdares may be treated to some unusual daytime sights—and some nerve-testing night sounds. They could be those of the hairy colobus monkey in the trees or, on occasions, that of a lone leopard as he causes consternation in the treetops stalking his favorite prey, the olive-backed baboon. When this happens, the baboon community suddenly comes alive.

A camp-out along the access road to the Ark—especially where clearings have been kept open—may at times produce rewarding sightings: a large herd of Cape buffalo taking a midday siesta, a small family group of shaggy-looking giant for-

est hogs rooting out plant tubers for lunch, or perhaps the stealthful crouch of a lioness about to pounce on a bushbuck. In a tent at night in some secluded spot, one may be in for an earful. Night sounds carry a long way, especially when the air is still. In such situations any nearby sound of a predatory molestation or killing can be a hair raiser. To some, sleeping under canvas in the bush is the supreme African experience.

But viewing from the lodges also has its moments of tension. Sometimes startling encounters take place at the water holes, causing consternation and mixed reactions among the onlookers. Visitors to the Ark have watched an unnerved female elephant driving her tusks into the side of a rhino, killing it, perhaps because it had come too close to her calf.

Ian Hardy of the Aberdare National Park staff reported a dramatic water hole episode at the Ark, an affair so moving that it merits partial reconstruction here. Those who were witnesses of the event, and there were many, will never forget it. It is a prime example of the fierce struggle for life that goes on in the African bush but is seldom played out before the eyes of visitors. The scenario read almost like a stage drama, the curtain rising at twilight, the stage a two-acre clearing with a half-acre water hole and boggy mudflats.

On this particular evening, according to Hardy, the stage was occupied by a pair of bushbuck and a family of giant forest hogs. The animals seemed cautious and alert, but eventually some began feeding while others licked the salt in an area halfway between the water's edge and some low bushes. At twilight the Ark's floodlights came on, casting an eerie brightness over the stage. The animals became skittish and one by one vanished into the rain forest. An uncanny, almost pal-

fig. 8. Giant forest hogs and buffalo crunch salt at the Ark water hole.

pable stillness settled over the empty, illuminated clearing.

Inside the Ark the guests, except for a few die-hards still on the observation decks, were enjoying sundowners and preparing for dinner. Unseen by anyone, a lone Cape buffalo propelled his way through a bamboo thicket en route to the clearing, probably bent on an hour's delightful sipping of salty ooze. Suddenly his ears folded back as the sounds of wild madness erupted behind him. He burst forward, dirt flying, front hooves digging into the moist ground. The din was the hunting chorus of excited hyenas—seven, although they sounded like more—close and very menacing.

The advancing night was filled with the whoops and weird wails of predators on the move.

The fleeing figure of a large beast so excited the hyenas that their yells rose to a crescendo. Lodge visitors began to return to the balconies. A small group with flash cameras raced down to the ground-level pillbox. The buffalo gained the advantage of the artificial moonlight clearing but not before one aggressor female grabbed his tail with her powerful jaws. She was dragged into the open before letting go.

Now the battleground could be seen from the Ark. Some onlookers grew nervous. The glowing eyes and watering mouths of the hyenas were so ominous to behold and the sounds of combat so unnerving as to be more than some guests could face. Several left. The grisly sight caused one woman to faint. Several people rushed to her aid, eventually carrying her off the balcony revived but visibly shaken.

The battle commenced at 6:36 P.M. An hour later the captain of the ship told his guests that the unpleasant affair might still last a long time. He deemed it wise for everyone to go inside, have dinner, and then go to bed. Asked by a dismayed guest why personnel did not drive the hyenas off, he shook his head. He acknowledged that life in the raw could be hard to watch but reminded visitors that they were in a national park, where staff were forbidden to interfere in such encounters.

The ordeal under the floodlights continued, accompanied by a steady stream of snorts, yaps, snarls, giggles, chuckles, and moans, along with deep-throated bovine bellows and wheezing. The hyena pack leader kept snapping at the buffalo's flanks, finally rushing in and emasculating the bull. Blood streamed down his legs. The oozing wound heightened the attackers' excitement. Three more hyenas leapt in and ripped out the tendons in the bull's rear legs. His rump sagged into the mud. The big prize was still dangerous, as each of the attackers knew. The battle continued.

At midnight a handful of guests remained on the upper deck. But now the interest had shifted to a herd of elephants emerging from the darkness on the far side of the water hole. Led by a large matriarch, they waited at the edge of clearing; then, sensing no danger to themselves, they plodded in single file toward the sipping holes. The elephants advanced to within ten yards of the combatants, paying them no heed, and began their night's siphoning of salt ooze.

The hyenas backed off momentarily. Half down, the buffalo was still panting and wheezing. The hyenas chuckled and giggled hungrily from a slight distance, saliva flowing from their jaws, eyes glowing fiercely in the eerie light. Soon the continuing vocal commotion seemed to be more annoyance than a self-respecting pachyderm could stand and the matriarch turned, trumpeted, and led her charges back into the dark night.

The hyenas leaped in again, savagely tearing away flesh. Then two hyenas fastened their fangs on the buffalo's throat and hung on. In minutes, the long saga was over, the prey suffocated. Immediately a furious feasting frenzy began. The warden checked the clock on the wall: it read 2:37 A.M.

The hyenas chomped away at the carcass until 4:30 A.M. when, fully gorged, they left the stage, bloody, mud-coated, bellies heavy and dragging. At daybreak the warden and six helpers went out to inspect the carnage. The buffalo was more than half devoured, disemboweled—a muddy, gory mess. The crew dragged the carcass to higher ground to avoid having it foul the water. Although hyenas are widely and mistakenly viewed as being purely scavengers, these animals had convincingly shown their effectiveness as hunters.

In the early evening the hyenas returned—all seven plus six additional members of their clan. Once again they feasted. Finally, with the edible portions of the carcass finished off, they slowly left the scene, bloody, bloated, and with bellies dragging again. For them it had been a rewarding hunt. As the glow of floodlights descended once more, the Ark and its darkening greenery became a peaceful world. Newly arrived visitors on the balconies had no idea of what had transpired on the quiet stage before them—deserted except for one lone rail that soon retreated from view.

Guests leaving the Ark after breakfast made a last-minute check of the log listing the animals that had visited the water hole at Treetops during the previous twenty-four hours: eleven elephants, ten Cape buffaloes, nine giant forest hogs, six warthogs, two giraffes, twenty-two olive-backed baboons, two bushbuck, and a bongo. At times, the log at the Ark lists similar sightings. Not bad for wildlife showing itself in one little clearing in the high rain forest of Kenya's Aberdare National Park.

Mount Kenya, in MOUNT KENYA NATIONAL PARK, is a natural stop after Treetops or the Ark. Almost every day from dawn to noon, the mountain's twin peaks and icy slopes sparkle with a come-hither look. The urge to go to the mountain, as with Kilimanjaro, is strong in many hearts.

There are several ways of getting there. One is to join a hiking group from the grounds of the remarkable Mount Kenya Safari Club near Nanyuki. Another is to get outfitted at the Mountain Lodge on the edge of the rain forest of Mount Kenya. The third, perhaps most commonly chosen, is to go to Naro Moru Lodge and get outfitted there, as this is right on the footslope of Mount Kenya and the journey from here is the shortest. The Naro has a beautiful setting with a variety of accommodations and features lovely walks, gardens, and a trout stream. Hiking gear and the services of guides and porters are available here. The lodge provides four-wheel-drive Land Rovers to the national park and on to Met Camp at

ten thousand feet above sea level. Here the road ends and the hiking trails begin.

It is a five-day trip from the Naro to Teleki Valley and back, including an overnight stop at Met Camp, a trek to Teleki Valley and a night at McKinder Camp in the valley, and then back to the Met, and finally a ride down the mountain to Naro Moru. The scenery is spectacular all the way and the foot travel after leaving the Met is arduous. This is a series of rough and deeply worn footpaths, virtually all upward, rather than a developed trail.

One crosses several life zones, from heavy bamboo forest into the moss-draped juniper and *Podocarpus* zone; heather and other heath plants predominate here as well. Red hot pokers show up everywhere at twelve thousand feet. Then comes the surprise, after a 1,500- to 1,800-foot climb over a wet, almost vertical bog, a zone of ledges and rocks and mud takes over. It is a six-hour crossing. Then the going levels off and leads to the delightful and picturesque Teleki Valley. Here Mount Kenya's twin peaks, Batian and Nelion, loom upward.

Big game, mostly elephant and buffalo, flourish in the wooded sectors. The leopard stalks all life zones from six thousand to eleven thousand feet. On rare occasions the elusive bongo and the even rarer okapi antelope may be spotted. Bird life is scarce, with the bateleur eagle sometimes seen at 11,500 feet.

Most hikers encountered on the mountain carry only light packs. Many are young and middle-aged German or Scandinavian adventurers. They may not be much on conversation but are eager to plod the trail. Less energetic spirits, usually American, often give up at the 12,500-foot level, especially if it rains, and heavy downpours are frequent. But the mountain offers scenic beauty all around plus occasional gorgeous sunsets, which make up for what wildlife hikers miss seeing by traveling on foot.

Encounters between people and big game do occur, however. One group of fifteen rain-soaked souls coming off the mountain below Met Camp after midnight in a single overloaded Land Rover came up against one bunch of buffaloes after another. The big beasts stopped in the middle of the road, defying the vehicle and its tense passengers. The animals finally chose to move on and the hikers departed without mishap.

CHAPTER 4

Avian Wonder Lakes of the Great Rift Valley

Much of the beauty, wonder, and fascination of Africa must be credited to its bird life. Birds can be seen virtually everywhere—in and around villages and towns, out on the open grasslands, in the bushveld, semiarid scrub, desert, wetlands, and swamps, along streams and rivers, and most notably around the many lakes of the Great Rift Valley.

While the primary interest of most visitors coming to Africa is big game, it is also true that birds rates high on the list for many. This is primarily because birds in Africa, in general, have high visibility. Central and South America and parts of the South Pacific may boast more species, but the heavy greenery in these tropical habitats makes birds much harder to see. Africa, for the most part, is more open and the feathered fraternity are easily seen. And those not visible can often be heard, as sound carries better in open terrain. The characteristic larger species, such as the ostrich, kori bustard, secretary bird, ground hornbill, flamingo, pelican, and the Old World vultures, storks, eagles, and hawks receive the most attention. A host of smaller birds to enjoy include the game birds, waterbirds, owls, kites, and the ever-present songbirds and insectivorous varieties. Altogether more than six hundred species and subspecies make up the extensive African-Ethiopian avifauna ecosystem.

The Great Rift Valley gives rise to an astonishing system of freshwater lakes, many of which are virtually inland seas. Some are large and deep, such as Lakes Malawi, Tanganyika, George, and Albert. There are also shallow lakes, some fresh and others with varying degrees of alkalinity. All attract birds. And where there are birds there are bird-watchers. However, because most visitors to East Africa are usually on a tight schedule, only a limited number of lakes can be included in one's itinerary. Among the smaller lakes nearest to Nairobi that seem a "must" are Naivasha, Bogoria, Nakuru, and Boringo. Tanzania also has several appealing lake destinations. Huge Lake Malawi lies further away; to see it may require a flight to Blantyre, Malawi.

LAKE NAIVASHA is a stunning lake and is essentially fresh; it features fishing, boating, and sailing. The Lake Naivasha Hotel has fascinating grounds, decked out in bright bougainvillea vines and other flowers. A boat trip to a nearby island gives the visitor a chance to hike around, see many cormorants, and watch small herds of almost tame waterbuck. The lake itself at times is the resting ground of hundreds of thousands of flamingos. As many as a million of the birds have been seen on the lake at one time, producing an aura of light pink as far as the eye could see. The flamingos do not come here to feed but rather to rest and drink, as they are not fish eaters. They depend on algae and small crustaceans for food.

To see flamingos feeding one must go to LAKE BOGORIA, several hours' driving distance away. Access to Bogoria is from two levels, a tree-lined upper ridge road or a lower road that follows the shoreline, now with an official gate to Lake Bogoria Nature Reserve. The upper road merits a stop some 200 yards above the lake. Here the view through the trees of the upper portion of the lake is an amazing sight—a shimmering panorama of white-pink bird-dom spread across half the lake surface. The strong, acrid odor of avian masses sharply pinches the nostrils. And the noise of birds is distinct.

If one's driver comes down the rough slope slowly and cautiously stops in the shelter of some yellow-barked fever trees, the avian spectacle that unfurls is unbelievably magical and mystical. The lake surface is a solid mat of flamingos, with great flocks taking off and others careening in clouds overhead. All the birds are flamingos. No other bird species can be seen. So packed are the birds on the water that takeoffs can only be conducted in groups, wave after wave slowly giving way to the next group. Here and there the astonishing scene is broken by plumes of steam rising from hot springs. Early visitors may find themselves the only human intrusion in the area. Imagine having a box seat in a secluded wilderness amphitheater while hundreds of thousands of flamingos perform an avian symphony right before your eyes. It is one of the world's great bird dramas— a bird-watcher's eden indeed.

The flamingos here and at other Rift lakes are members of the only two species in Africa, readily told apart by size. The greater flamingo is almost twice as large as the lesser flamingo but their coloration is virtually the same except for the bill. Greater flamingos have both black and pink on their bills while the lesser flamingo's bill is entirely black. Although both species have pink feet, the birds when massed generally appear more whitish than pink, the latter shade coming mostly from the wings, which are edged with black. American flamingos, in contrast, are predominantly pink with only some black showing. The New World has four species: the American, Chilean, Andean, and the James. The two African species, however, represent the largest and the smallest of the six kinds.

In watching the flocks at Bogoria it quickly becomes clear that the lessers outnumber the greaters by more than fifty to one; moreover, they appear to be feeding on different foods. Research has shown this to be so. The more numerous lesser flamingos are vegetarians, subsisting on algae, while the greaters are carnivores, feeding on microscopic animals, such as copepods (minute shrimplike creatures), lake-fly larvae, and similar organisms. Thus the two African species live together side by side without competing for food.

When feeding on algae, the lessers strain their food through a sieve in the mandible. The greaters also strain their animal food, squeezing out the soda water and swallowing what is nutritious. Bogoria is one of a number of soda lakes, lakes high in alkaline mineral deposits.

Scientists estimate that there are today roughly six million flamingos in the world and that Africa can claim about half this number. When a million birds suddenly congregate on one lake or several, how is it that they do not eat themselves out of house and home? One answer is that the soda lakes are so rich in nutrients that large populations of flamingos can be sustained without endangering the basic food supply. Algae, for example, multiply rapidly in tropical waters, and when heavy bird excrement is added to such waters, a rich soup of algae is produced. The same can be said for the tiny crustaceans on which the greater flamingos feed. Thus in a way the birds help perpetuate their own nourishment.

Most soda lakes in East Africa are so caustic (from mineral deposits) that fish cannot live in them. Were flamingos fish eaters, certain lakes would soon be exhausted of food. If one reason for the birds' great numbers is the abundance of primitive plants and animals in soda waters, another is that few other species of birds are plant feeders, and the lesser flamingos hence have the lake food supply pretty much to themselves. Moreover, the African flamingo is little affected by civilization. African people do not eat these birds and seldom go to the soda lakes because of the lack of fish. Also, people cannot drink the caustic water or otherwise use it in agriculture.

Facing no competition with people, the flamingos flourish, despite being a considerable draw for predators. Tawny eagles and marabou storks prey on the young, weak, old, sick, or crippled. In some places, such as in the waters of famous Ngorongoro Crater in Tanzania, spotted hyenas take their toll. And floods raise havoc with flamingo nesting sites. Too much hot, dry weather can hurt the eggs, affect incubation, and injure chicks.

At Lake Bogoria there are many hot springs and the birds gather around them eagerly as these waters, though hot, are fresh and can be drunk safely. Lake Hennington, some forty miles west of Lake Nakuru, also has freshwater hot springs where flamingos congregate. In the far western Rift such huge lakes as George and Albert attract the birds mainly for resting and drinking.

One leaves Bogoria reluctantly; the flamingos seem to hold one under a spell, often for too long to make Lake Nakuru by evening. The shoreline on both portions of the lake, the upper and lower, frequently offers other wildlife: tawny eagles in pairs in acacia trees, warthog, groups of waterbuck grazing and looking up, and inquisitive giraffe halting to check out visitors.

The run to LAKE NAKURU takes less than two hours. Here vervet monkeys beg for a handout. While feeding wild animals is prohibited in parks, monkeys and baboons have an engaging way of persuading people to wink at the rules. As one progresses into the park, impala cross the road and are visible in the headlights. They seem unhurried, feeling safe, and hardly give vehicles so much as a glance. Groups of waterbuck peer out intently from darkening clearings near the road, but presently they too choose to ignore all vehicles and continue feeding. As we approached Lion Hill Camp, the elegant heads of two giraffes protruded above the branches of an umbrella acacia against the fading skyline. In short, our welcome to one of the Rift's foremost wildlife sanctuaries held satisfying wildlife sightings in the advancing twilight.

After getting assigned to one of the cottages perched in neat rows on a hillside, guests enjoy a festive candlelight dinner in an open-sided dining tent. Later, people gather around a joyous outside bonfire to sip nightcaps and exchange some quiet safari talk before retreating to bed.

Sleep may not always be without disturbance, however. On our visit, around midnight, with everyone fast asleep, all hell suddenly broke loose as violent shrieks erupted in the bush above the camp. It sounded as if an operatic soprano were being strangled. "Sounds like a Texas tomcat," murmured one cottage occupant. In a sanctuary noted for birds, it did seem unusual. No lions are present here now, despite the camp's name, but leopards are common. We surmised that the fracas could have been a leopard taking a baboon, its favorite prey. Baboons are plentiful at Nakuru.

Lake Nakuru was proclaimed a national park soon after independence came to Kenya. On August 29, 1973, H.R.H. Prince Bernhard of Holland, then president of the World Wildlife Fund, presented Kenya's president, Jomo Kenyatta, with a check for the equivalent of $210,000 to ensure the success and future of this remarkable bird sanctuary and to increase its size from 14,261 acres to 42,549 acres. The move heralded one of the most notable conservation achievements in East Africa. Children from all over the continent and in Europe collected money for the project. Today the world is assured that at least one prominent soda lake in East Africa will continue to remain a haven for flamingos and other waterbirds for years to come. More recently a fenced rhino reserve was added.

Most visitors who stay at Lion Hill Camp take a minibus tour around Lake Nakuru. Usually at the start of the tour a number of wildlife species put in an appearance: impala, waterbuck, and Cape buffalo. Along the dirt road near camp are a few of the strange large euphorbia known as the candelabra tree, and later the circuit passes a hillside packed with them, a stunning view of a bizarre forest bathed in midmorning sunlight.

The candelabra tree, *Euphorbia ingens,* resembles the giant Mexican organpipe cactus, but in reality it is not a cactus. The trunk is fluted, has many branches, and indeed has the shape of a giant candelabrum. The species can be distinguished from a cactus by its peculiar milky sap and by the fact that its spines occur singly or in pairs. Only a few of the more than two thousand euphorbia species in the world attain heights of thirty feet or more, among them the picturesque candelabra of Nakuru. Anyone coming in contact with the sap soon discovers painful blisters forming on the skin. It is said that natives often toss cut branches of the tree into a lake and the oozing milky sap quickly paralyzes fish, thus making fishing easy.

Down along the lakeshore reedbuck may be spotted. A pair may be poised at the water's edge, ready to make their characteristic whistling leap. Light-colored and somewhat yellowish in overall appearance, they are smaller than impala, weighing perhaps less than eighty pounds. The whistling sound is said to come from the squeezing of the inguinal pouch as the animal begins its leap.

Lake Nakuru being only moderately alkaline, birds of many species come here to feed on its aquatic life and to rest. Roger Tory Peterson, dean of American ornithologists and world-famous bird artist, has described Lake Nakuru as providing "the greatest ornithological spectacle on earth." Most tours around the lake bring sightings of flocks of flamingos and other waterbirds coming and going—both species of flamingos, pelicans, yellow-billed storks, egrets, herons, ducks, and coots. At times almost the entire lake is a mass of fluttering wings. Other birds seen on or around the lake include the marabou stork, usually seen singly, plus kingfishers, avocets, spoonbills, and sandpipers. Bird lovers can spend days watching and studying birds and never get bored for a single minute.

While flamingos can be seen around many lakes in East Africa, and at times even in the rain-filled pans of the Kalahari desert in Botswana, their breeding places are seldom seen because they often select inhospitable sites in which to nest. Occasional nest building and even egg laying has been seen at Lake Nakuru, but for the most part the flamingos breed elsewhere. The only greater flamingo breeding ground within easy reach in East Africa is on a small lake in Kenya in the Great Rift Valley. The grounds, however, are in private ownership.

The lesser flamingo, however, is a breeder on the far-off islands and mudflats of Lake Natron in northern Tanzania. To reach the nesting colonies, usually invisible from shore because of haze and shimmering heat, the investigator must struggle on foot over mudflats and alkaloid ooze for hours. Such forays can be hazardous. Leslie Brown, a Nairobi naturalist and bird observer, once made such a trip to the nesting colonies and in so doing got soda crust in his boots, resulting in serious burns. He almost lost both feet from alkaloid inflammation and was laid up for weeks.

Flamingos lay one to two eggs in a conical nest made of mud and sand. Both parents help with the incubation, which lasts from twenty-eight to thirty-two days. Four days after hatching, the young begin to follow their parents and after seventy-eight days they are able to fly. Parents feed the newborn chicks by regurgitating partially digested food into the mouths of the young. Once the chicks hatch, how can the parents returning from feeding forays recognize their own offspring with so many look-alikes around? Greater flamingos have been closely studied, but the answer remains unclear.

Another mystery yet unsolved is the question of why flamingos suddenly leave one feeding lake in favor of another; speculation is that such switches have to do with food supplies. Most mass movements occur at night. Thus, one evening there may be a million birds resting on a lake, and in the morning they are gone—perhaps to Nakuru or Hennington or Bogoria. Sometimes they migrate long distances northward and may not be reported until they reach Lake Turkana in northernmost Kenya; others may move south to Lake Buenavelo in Zambia or go to the great Makgadikgadi pans in Botswana. Still others may fly all the way to the Etosha Pan in Namibia.

In the intensely alkaloid waters where lesser flamingos breed, one mystery in the life of the young has been revealed. To observers flying over Lake Natron—where thousands of chicks have been studied regularly on the soda mudflats—some birds appeared to be slower and weaker than the rest, their legs heavily encrusted with soda-pasted anklets. Observers in a small plane noticed several tawny eagles waiting around for a chance to make an easy kill. Any flightless chicks unable to keep up with the masses, and especially those weighted down with heavy soda anklets, were easy prey for the eagles. Those that had gained their feathers and were able to fly away to safety would soon have their anklets dissolved in freshwater. Many young, however, never make it. Those reaching adulthood without mishap often live a long time, sometimes as much as eighty years.

New developments at the noted bird sanctuary of Lake Nakuru involve an attempt to bring back one member of the big five, the black rhino, to a Kenya national park from which it had been exterminated. This experiment is part of a series of small, intensively patrolled rhino sanctuaries throughout Africa. Scientists and conservation workers seeking a location where an experimental project might succeed came up with Lake Nakuru as the best site. The park already had Cape buffalo, giraffe, impala, waterbuck, other antelope, and leopard. Hopes are that by bringing in a breeding group of black rhinos, a small population of the endangered large beasts may be built up. Being close to the city of Nakuru, the animals would have to be closely guarded against poachers. The plan called for an extensive fencing project, aided by the World Wildlife Fund. The fencing complete, fifteen black rhinos were brought in. Now it remains to be seen if the experiment will succeed. To help ensure the long-term success of the project, an extensive educational campaign, both local and nationwide, also was launched. The rhino experiment at Nakuru is being closely watched by wildlife conservationists all over the world. Can the illegal killing of endangered species in Africa be prevented here? Time will tell.

LAKE BORINGO, near Lake Bogoria but some distance from Nakuru, is another freshwater Rift Valley lake where waterbirds congregate.

Many hippos are also seen here. While Boringo offers sport fishing, boating, and sailing, the chief attraction here is birds, with the pink-backed pelican a noted drawing card. The pelican is one of Africa's largest birds. When its dip-net pouch is included, it looks even bigger. Adults measure 44 to 54 inches in length, exclusive of the huge bill, which averages 14 inches in length. Of the six species known, all are white except the seashore-inhabiting brown pelican, which is found in America. The four Old World species are distributed in Europe, Asia, Africa, and Australia.

Lake Boringo is quite a large lake with small rocky volcanic islands protruding here and there. Some years ago a group decided to turn one isolated island into a bird-watchers' camp and called it Island Camp. Rough and rocky, the small island has many steps leading to various facilities and a series of tents perched overlooking its promontories. Visitors come by boat and are virtually isolated from civilization, except by radio. If there ever was a Shangri-la for bird lovers in Africa, this is it. During the day dozens of species of waterbirds can be seen flying past the camp. Several pairs of fish eagles call all day long. At times along the shore of this islet, sand grouse can be seen wetting their underfeathers so as to carrying small globs of moisture to their chicks located far away. Both parents do this until the young are fledged and can fly and get water on their own.

At night after most guests have sipped a nightcap and a few have crawled into their nests of canvas, suddenly one can hear them—flamingos! They are honking like Canada geese and flying in a V-shaped formation against the backdrop of a rising moon. Perhaps headed north to faraway Lake Turkana, or turning and heading south to

Lake Malawi after a stopover in Tanzania's Lake Manyara, they are in any event bidding farewell to Island Camp and its small birdwatching group. Overhead in a fig tree above the site of the highest tents perched on a rocky promontory, a diminutive owl sings out its melancholy notes; wafting in on a light breeze come the satisfying grunts of distant hippos feeding in some lush greenery. The avian eden of Lake Boringo has shown its best and finally succumbs to slumber.

LAKE MALAWI, one of the huge Rift Valley lakes in the south, is an incredible place. Although a little hard to get to by minivan or even aircraft, it more than compensates for its isolation. Formerly called Lake Nyasa, it was named by the explorer David Livingstone when he reconnoitered the beautiful Shire Highlands.

Lake Malawi is the southernmost large lake of the Great Rift Valley, running to a depth of 2,310 feet and stretching fully 363 miles in length. It is especially famous for its more than two hundred kinds of freshwater fish, 80 percent of which are landlocked and endemic. The chief most common species is the tilapia, which attracts many waterbirds and fish eagles.

The fish eagle is an omnipresent bird of prey, found wherever freshwaters and fish are present. White-headed, the fish eagle resembles the American bald eagle; like the osprey or fish hawk but larger, fish eagles are masters at fishing. To witness fish eagles diving for fish when the food supply is abundant and avian territorial limits are extremely restricted is to gain a new appreciation for these remarkable birds of prey.

Fish eagles stage impressive flying maneuvers during courtship, which lasts for days or even weeks. They twist, soar, dive, roll, touch wings. They call out amorous love cries to one another. Finally, when a bond is made, a joyous mating period follows, along with nest building. Often a mated pair will use the same nest over and over again, each spring adding a few sticks. The female lays from one to three eggs, with incubation performed by both parents, each brooding while the other goes out to fish. Pairs are made with great caution, and when they mate, it is for life.

The young hatch in about thirty days, after which the adults' fishing forays must intensify if they are to feed their growing young effectively. Again the parents both work at it. With this kind of serious attention, the young grow rapidly, but invariably some chicks become stronger than others. The weak often die from hunger and heat. Starvation is caused by, of all things, the wind. When southeasterly winds blow hard for days, the lake surface becomes so roiled up and its waters so choppy that the fish retreat to the depths. The eagles then must wait it out or fly long distances to other waters for food. The result is that only the strongest of the young survive. Usually by the time the young are ready to fly and leave the nest, only one strong young bird is left.

When the tilapia are abundant and near the surface, the eagles have a ball. They eye their prey from a hundred feet above, then drop at a sharp angle, make a quick dive with talons extended, grab a fish, and are off. Not all dives are successful but many are. When a catch is made, it is a winged symphony of power, elegance, and control.

For many people, this bird's quavering, commonly heard cry is symbolic of the wild spirit of Africa.

CHAPTER 5

The Seething Plains of Serengeti and Masai Mara

The plains! How the very thought of them makes the adrenaline rise and the heart pound with pleasurable anticipation. It is a world completely unto itself with an abundance of life so rich and diversified that one has to see it to believe it. It is a land of wonders—high, overpowering skies and long uninterrupted vistas, strong ultraviolet rays and intense sunlight, hot noontime temperatures, and often weeks and months without a drop of rain. There are days before the seasonal rains when great cumulus clouds appear, and breaks in them allow sunlit openings to cast variegated shadows to race across the landscape. Mostly, however, the plains are a special grassland called savannah, which sustains unbelievable hordes of wild grazing animals and their predators. It is in essence a page from the Pleistocene, a window on the African past, its force perhaps enhanced because we sense its profusion as an emanation from our own evolutionary past, which we now have the power to conserve or destroy.

The epitome of the savannah in East Africa is the Serengeti–Masai Mara grassland ecosystem in northern Tanzania and south-central Kenya. It comprises the principal parade ground of the wildebeest and zebra plus their associated migratory herbivores. All of the big five species occur here—elephant, rhinoceros, buffalo, lion, and leopard. The first three occupy restricted ranges and thus do not migrate. The two predators and other carnivores have scattered territories throughout the ecosystem but do not join the migrants for long distances.

The Serengeti ecosystem embraces not only Tanzania's famous 3,200,000-acre Serengeti National Park but also the Ngorongoro Crater Conservation Area in northeastern Tanzania and the Masai Mara Game Preserve, 700,000 acres of savannah extending into southern Kenya.

What are the plains like on a typical December afternoon when the grazers pass in review before a protruding granite hillock? A single square mile of tropical grassland may show incredible herds of wildebeest on the move, grunting,

fig. 9. The solitary leopard, normally a night hunter, slinks through the grass by daylight.

reminiscent of migrating caribou on the northern barrens of Canada and Alaska's Arctic National Wildlife Range. An estimate may put the number of wildebeest in view at between nineteen and twenty thousand. In and around openings there may be fifteen hundred to two thousand Burchell's zebras, their high-pitched voices sounding more like barking dogs than like wild equines. Plump looking and seemingly well fed, they reach down and bite off grasses as they move. Then may come more wildebeest and with them groups of other antelope: topi, hartebeest, eland, impala, and gazelles. They move about and also snip away grass.

In the procession are stately giraffes, their heads protruding over the tops of umbrella acacias in ones and twos. Gangs of baboons move nervously, picking away at tender morsels. And scattered about are individuals and groups of Grant's gazelles and their lesser counterparts, the Thomson's gazelles, which trot around daintily with windshield-wiper tails forever working away back and forth. Birds, too, help give the savannah vibrant life—ostrich, kori bustard, secretary bird, a pair of ground hornbills, storks, cranes, egrets, and a host of smaller species. The steady cooing of doves and the cawing of pied crows issue from nearby and distant coverts. All in all it is a wonderfully lively pageant. Scientists who have seriously studied the savannah go a step further and say it is the most endowed realm of wild nature on the face of our earth.

The Serengeti savannah is not all endless stretches of flat or undulating grassland. It is punctuated with secondary environments created by the physiography of the land, producing a vivid mosaic of habitats all across the plains—water holes here and there, low places with intermittent streams, swales lined with lemon-colored fever trees, and patches of open woodland where shade is more plentiful and heavy growth of tall grasses makes good haunts for leopard and lion. Scattered throughout the Serengeti too are strange-looking granite hills, called *kopjes,* where predators often lie and watch the slow passage of prey animals. At a distance the kopjes look like a morning crop of fresh mushrooms suddenly sprouting in a vast green pasture. They protrude through the surrounding landscape, which consists of hundreds of feet of rich silt and sand and mud and volcanic ash, producing some of the richest soils on earth. The Serengeti-Mara stronghold also features a few permanent watercourses of which the Mara River, originating in the Masai Mara Game Preserve and flowing through northern Tanzania to Lake Victoria, is the most vital in the area.

In the plains, much of the animal activity is geared to and timed by the rains, everything from the hatching of fairy shrimp eggs in rock pools on the kopjes to the migration of the wildebeest. The coming of the rains also awakens a sand-entombed beetle, the dry riverbed turtle, and the spadefoot toad. They have remained buried in the mud for many months.

The rains in the Serengeti-Mara come in two phases, the short rains of November and December and the longer, more copious rains of April,

May, and early June. And of course it is the rains that bring on the grass and browse, the plants that basically sustain the animal life. Grasses are the key. In the eastern plains, short grasses predominate. In the central plains, grasses of medium height are more common. And in the western savannah, tall grasses are the rule.

Low places often display water holes and intermittent streams, which support fever trees—smooth, yellowish-barked acacias that are a habitat of the leopard. The trees were once thought to cause malaria, but science eventually pinpointed the Anopheles mosquito as the carrier of the disease; their connection with fever trees is merely that they breed in the same moist places where these trees grow.

Lions favor the swales and riverine woodlands for shade at midday, although any shade will do, even a parked vehicle with nervous tourists waiting. Lion prides also like to rest under shady lone umbrella acacias, which may be in some demand by other predators too. Leopards often drag a kill up a tree to save it from marauding lions or hyenas.

To see lions in the shade of a tree during the heat of the day seems a paradox—the savage king of beasts reclining and often ridiculously lolling in a manner most unbecoming for an efficient carnivore. With all four feet in the air and a huge maned head resting on the ground, eyes closed, the mighty king looks anything but the embodiment of power. Lionesses reposing indolently, and with perhaps only three or four cubs alert, the lion pride appears to be the very antithesis of ferocity. But make no mistake. When prey come close or if people annoy the group, in a split second lions can turn on an explosive response of ferocious energy. Lions spend only 15 percent of their time

fig. 10. A lioness laps up water.

in hunting and eating; the other 85 percent is chiefly devoted to lassitude and resting, attesting to their great efficiency as predators.

While the Serengeti-Mara stronghold is distinguished for its teeming large mammals, its bird life is also very rich. Bird life here is formally known as part of the Ethiopian avifauna, which features more than four hundred resident and migratory species and includes the world's largest flightless bird, the ostrich; East Africa's biggest bird of prey, the black vulture; and one of the world's great flying birds, the marabou stork, the wingspan of which may exceed that of the famous wandering albatross of the South Seas. Out on the plains the observer also sees dozens of species of colorful songbirds and insectivorous species. Present at times are flamingos, both lesser and greater, guinea fowl, sand grouse, doves, hawks, and several eagle species.

In the winter, geese fly in from Egypt, and storks sail in from such distant places as Poland and Russia. Year in and year out, the plains of the Serengeti and Mara are alive with avian denizens, often displaying in the air and on the ground, as in the twirling and bowing of the male ostrich before its mate, and the waltzing and fretting of the sand grouse during mating time. While a seasonal migration of birds to or from the plains is evident, the contrast in bird numbers and activities through the seasons scarcely damages viewing as many species are present in the grasslands all year long. Much activity is tied directly to the migrating herbivores, which not only stir up an abundance of food but contribute to the richness of the plains with their own dung.

Everyone on safari, of course, is most anxious to see the spectacle of the migrating herds. So the inevitable question arises: When is the best time to see this drama and where? Exact dates do not matter much, for the animals are out on the plains, somewhere, all the time. Any responsible tour operator can plan an itinerary favoring the migration. However, it can be helpful to have a general idea of the seasonal events that take place.

On the lower Serengeti in early July, the grasslands have already reached maturity and are starting to turn golden. Even the taller grasses under the thorn trees are beginning to yellow. Two months have passed since the plains have had any measurable rain, and the grazing animals know it. The wildebeest in particular are aware of what is happening and, together with other antelope, such as Grant's gazelle, Thomson's gazelle, and topi, commence to trek toward the higher, greener, unused pastures. At one point some dark columns turn eastward toward the Ngorongoro Crater. Others head northward toward Kenya's Masai Mara.

The wildebeest form long, continuous bands, sometimes led by an aggressive bull wildebeest, occasionally by a big zebra stallion. The great migration is on. As new grasslands are reached, the bands open up and spread out, flooding the plains with thousands of restless, grunting wildebeest. The wildebeest calves by now are four to five months old and are forever trying to keep up with their mothers. Some young are lost; others are trampled to death, their remains quickly picked

up by hyenas and vultures. Some young are lost in fires. When the land is shorn of grass, like a freshly mown lawn, the animals move on; always, however, their course is toward newer pastures, fresher grasses, and higher terrain, their direction somehow communicated to them by means not clear to us.

As the procession of noisy ungulates creeps across the plains there are flesh eaters on the move seeking to intercept them—lions, hyenas, a cheetah or two, or a lone leopard. On rare occasions, wild dogs appear. The various predators do not join the cavalcade of grazers for long distances as they have home territories and must confine their hunting to these in order to avoid encroaching on neighbors' hunting terrain, which carries sanctions. In general the limits of predators are so well spaced that the grazers are forever crossing the grounds of the meat hunters. It is estimated that in the Serengeti National Park there are about five thousand lions, indicating the presence of lion prides throughout the Serengeti-Mara ecosystem.

Lions hunt in groups in a cooperative manner with the lionesses doing most of the killing, the attacks generally coming from ambush. The usual method of killing is by suffocation, grabbing the animal by the muzzle or throat. Often when a kill is made, however, the territorial male muscles in and drives the females and cubs away. He feasts first. At other times feeding is a general free-for-all. Not infrequently a group of hyenas drives a lioness from her kill; sometimes even scaring off several lions from a carcass. However, several lions together may rob hyenas of their kills too; efficient group hunters, hyenas often catch and dispatch their own prey.

Wild dogs, now exceedingly scarce, hunt in packs. They characteristically pursue the herds

fig. 11. Only the strongest and healthiest male lions dominate the pride.

short distances and then pick out a victim and run it down, killing it by degrees in a cooperative attack, often disemboweling their prey and feeding while the animal is still alive. Although this is gruesome to watch, the animals are adapted to killing this way, lacking the size and strangling power of larger predators. It makes wild dogs seem especially savage, until one learns how wonderfully solicitous of their young they are and how complex and intricate their social organization is.

Cheetahs hunt alone or in pairs, usually in daylight, their technique being to run down a victim, bite at the throat, and then suffocate it. The leopard, in contrast, is mostly a solitary night hunter depending on stealth, quick seizure, and mortal bites for its kills.

George Schaller, a noted wildlife biologist who spent several years studying predators and prey in the Serengeti, has revealed that many of our established notions about predators are not backed up by facts. Lions, for example, do not necessarily prey purely on the old, sick, or weak but take what comes most easily and surely, be it a confused mature zebra or a newborn wildebeest calf. The weak, old, injured, and very young are taken in disproportionate numbers only because they

Masai men dancing
near Nairobi, Kenya.

Crossing the Athi
River in a rubber raft.

Many East African
lodge gardens are
a riot of bright
bougainvilleas.

A group of tourists climbing Mount Kenya at 12,000 feet.

Defiant Cape buffalo are met on Mount Kenya.

Wildebeest drown in the Mara River when crossing.

A Lake Manyara tree-climbing lion.

Two cheetahs attack
and kill a wildebeest
in the crater.

Female ostrich with
young on the open
savannah.

The klipspringer is a
remarkable jumper.

Victoria Falls on the
Zambezi River.

A crocodile on a sandbar on the Ewaso Ng'iro.

Ugandan boys frolic on a termite castle.

present predators with opportunity proportionally more than do healthy adults.

As the migrating hordes move on and no rains fall, the shorn grasses grow dry and fires break out; many burn for days. The flames consume what grasses remain, then burn small saplings, trees, old stumps. Ahead of the flames it is common to see large birds avidly feeding. Ground hornbill, kori bustards, and secretary birds are after escaping snakes, lizards, and insects. The fires in the Masai Mara are mostly set by local people to burn off old stubble and make way for new grass for their cattle. This is especially common with the Masai in the Mara and in the Ngorongoro. Other fires are accidentally started by careless people and many are set by lightning.

Ecologically, however, fires and grasslands go together. This is one reason why the savannah abounds with game. The fires destroy the standing forage, but the long-term benefits are such that vast areas of tropical scrubland are kept open as savannah.

The restless migrants are steadily on the move carrying out their life's processes of feeding, staking out breeding zones, fighting for females, mating, carrying young, and giving birth. Constantly eating, always on the go, the animals fill the Serengeti plains, choking the national park's 5,600 square miles, only to spill out over its borders on long-established routes, guided by instincts developed during eons of roaming over a range more like ten thousand square miles to take best advantage of seasonal pasture.

The most abundant species in the Serengeti vary in number from time to time. A recent count shows that there are now some 1,000,000 to 1,500,000 wildebeest; 180,000 to 240,000 Thomson's gazelle; 150,000 zebra; 65,000 impala;

50,000 buffalo; and 25,000 topi. So numerous are the animals in some areas of the plains that the observer is never out of sight of them.

One February afternoon in the central Serengeti, the small group with whom I was traveling ran into a large concentration of game and decided to make a count. In one two-mile stretch of dirt track near the Seronera Wildlife Lodge, our tally showed 4,276 wildebeest, 2,970 Thomson's gazelle, 1,842 zebra, and, surprisingly, 806 giraffe. Normally giraffe are nowhere near that concentrated on the plains, but at that time they were bunched up in considerable numbers.

On another occasion, this time in August in the Mara, we encountered a huge migration of wildebeest and zebra. The place this time was Governor's Camp on the Mara River. Here in a half-mile stretch of savannah we tallied around seventy thousand wildebeest and thirty-eight thousand zebra. Wildebeest darkened the plains like a black cloud. Herds of zebra milled noisily around everywhere. Thousands of Thomson's gazelle covered open areas, some walking singly, others in scattered groups, their little tails as always working energetically. These tiny antelope, called tommies, are captivating to watch. At times, too, we ran into large jumping herds of impala. These graceful antelope are so agile that if pressed they can leap right over a minibus, making single bounds of thirty feet or more.

Scattered among the vast herds were also bands of topi antelope, their reddish coats glistening in the sunlight, their strange-looking horns swept back in odd fashion. A few males here and there occupied separate termite mounds where they served as lookouts for their own kind as well as for other antelope.

At one point we spotted a huge phalanx of large

fig. 12. Burchell's zebra on the great African savannah.

black beasts approaching, perhaps as many as three hundred, and we moved closer, then halted. The Cape buffalo presently stopped too, their massive heads turned menacingly toward us. Suddenly a big bull broke the stare and bounded forward, triggering the rest of the column into a dust-billowing stampede. The rumble from their pounding hooves sounded like thunder rolling over the nearby Lioto Hills.

One personal encounter with wildebeest I will never forget. Thousands were amassing beside the Mara River near Governor's Camp in Kenya, preparing to cross the fifty-yard-wide swollen river. In an open Land Rover we rolled right into the midst of the masses and stopped. Some animals came so close that we could touch them. It was an eyeball-to-eyeball encounter, with untold numbers of gnus grunting all around us. Mixed with the smell of torn earth was the acrid odor of dung and urine, so strong that we could stand it for only half an hour. Here and there under pounding feet were a number of calves trampled to death by the moving hordes. On the riverbank hundreds of beasts could be seen leaping into the river in a desperate attempt to cross. But the banks were high and slippery and the river so full and swift that for many the effort to cross proved fruitless. Bellowing gnus that reached the opposite bank fell back into the water repeatedly and drowned. It was a daylight nightmare of hell.

Two hours later and about a thousand yards farther down on the river, the tragedy of ill-fated crossings was almost too much for an experienced wildlife biologist to bear: we saw masses of drowned wildebeest floating downriver in the current, victims of attempted crossings upstream. So many dead animals rafted downriver that one could have ridden on them. Some were hung up on rocks and logs. Then came another incredible sight. On both riverbanks we spotted huge concentrations of vultures. They had assembled in astonishing numbers, the largest gathering in a clearing on the opposite side. The magnitude of this bird aggregation was beyond description. No one would dream so many scavengers could assemble in one place at one time. We estimated the flock at about five thousand. It looked as if all the griffin vultures in Kenya had come to the Mara for a grand feast.

Crocodiles were in the river too, dozens of huge ones, many visibly gulping down wildebeest flesh. Hippos also rolled in the water, barreling about like huge wine kegs, surfacing their big rufous heads to breathe, and filling the air with their characteristic loud series of snorts. Meanwhile, upriver, more columns of hard-pressed wildebeest were leaping wildly into the water. More and more jumped, hurling themselves desperately into the river, pressed from behind by an irresistible force. So far as we knew all perished in the river. Where we were on the lower riverbank, we could still hear the death moans and screams of the dying. We walked a short distance to the river to take more photographs but the advancing, hissing thousands of vultures appeared so menacing that we decided to return to the Land Rover. For

us the Armageddon on the Mara was enough for one afternoon's game drive.

That evening around the bar at camp we talked with the camp director about the drownings. He said that the river takes its share of the beasts, but that we should be here in late December when the rains come and the wildebeest begin returning from their northern pastures. So many thousands die then, it's unbelievable, he said. The waters of the Mara run higher then and many more wildebeest die. So many drown, in fact, that their carcasses actually dam up the river.

Such decimation of the herds by drowning in rivers and shallow lakes is one of nature's ways of keeping the vast herds in balance with their food supply. With 150,000 to 200,000 calves born each year, it is obvious that something must take the excess or the Serengeti-Mara plains would be overrun with wildebeest. Predators take their share, and surely starvation, injury, and disease take their toll. But one suspects that the greatest number of wildebeest die by drowning in the rivers and lakes that are the greatest obstacles to their migration on the great plains.

The Serengeti-Mara spectacle is a year-round continuous drama of wildebeest and other herbivores ever on the move in search of food. Some wildebeest travel as much as a thousand miles in their seasonal cycle. During these extensive journeys over the plains the gnus carry out all kinds of strange rituals. During the May rutting season when the wildebeest are on the lower plains, mostly in Tanzania, a whole repertoire of antics takes place. Bulls prance around as if crazy, jumping, running in circles, loping like wild horses; many perform showy acrobatics before the females, which stand around looking bored. The great turnaround takes place in late June and July when the big trek out of the hot, dry, dusty Serengeti begins once more.

By midsummer the long lines out on the central plains divide. One stream of animals heads for the upper extension of the Serengeti, into Kenya's Masai Mara. Others veer toward the greener pastures of the Ngorongoro Crater Conservation Area. Some groups actually climb up the crater highlands and descend into the grassland inside the crater itself. Others remain in the area until the grass is cropped low and instinct tells them it is time to start moving again—back toward the lower plains—back to new life and new beginnings.

As the stupendous herds play out their annual cavalcade, the grazers perform a remarkable division of labor: Tommies and other gazelles clip down the tenderest grasses; wildebeest, impala, and topi seek out the midlevel grasses; buffalo, rhino, and zebra take the coarse grasses and weeds. And elephants go for the tall grasses and the leaves, twigs, and bark of shrubs and trees. Giraffes browse away among the high acacias, moving from one thornbush grove to another, browsing from tree to tree.

As the large mammals move through, no part of the savannah is grazed down to the bare earth, as one sees often with confined domestic cattle. Thus the utilization of the savannah is efficient, complete, and without waste or damage.

Truly, then, the yearly migration has reached full circle—a cycle of animal survival ritual that has no real beginning and no end.

CHAPTER 6

Olduvai, Manyara, and Ngorongoro

SINGULAR WORLDS APART

After the high adventure on the great plains some might welcome a change of pace as well as scenery. A visit to the volcanic highlands is a tantalizing option. Here three significant but different realms of nature beckon strongly: Olduvai Gorge, Lake Manyara National Park, and Ngorongoro Crater. Each rates as a world apart and, ecologically, comprises a microcosm all its own. These three places, though very different, all have in common—in contrast to the plains and the big lakes—a kind of intimacy in the landscape: that sense of connection to antiquity at Olduvai, the enclosed quality of Ngorongoro, the nature of viewing wildlife in a microcosm at Manyara.

OLDUVAI GORGE in the eastern Serengeti in Tanzania is not what most travelers would call an overwhelming piece of real estate, especially when one first sees it—a large, dry depression with sparse vegetation, with low surrounding cliffs, and without as much wildlife as other areas promise. The locals call it a *donga,* but to an American eye

it is a semiarid valley reminiscent of several in the U.S. West, for example in Colorado's Mesa Verde National Park, only much less spectacular. What is important here is not the scenery, for other sights in East Africa surpass it a hundredfold. The small interpretive museum at the site is not impressive—a modest structure perched in stark isolation on the edge of a small escarpment, as if waiting forlornly for infrequent visitors. Nor is the egglike, metallic-looking dinosaur fossil very exciting as it rests mounted on a pedestal near the building, but it gives one a clue. What is noteworthy here is what was found here—the fossils of early humans, which electrified the world and made anthropological history.

Two million years ago, scientists claim, Olduvai Gorge contained small lakes and a large, steaming swamp. The place was overshadowed by two extinct volcanoes, one of which today is known as the Ngorongoro Crater. The climate at the time was hotter and more humid than now.

In that lush green valley there roamed ancestral antelope, wild long-haired pig, a prehistoric baboon, and several types of gazelle. Huge lammergeyers, or bearded vultures, soared aloft and flamingos fluttered around the shallow lakes by the millions. The largest herbivores included the elephantlike dinotherium that fed in the marshes as well as a strange tree-cropping caleocothere and an oddly antlered siwantherium, something akin to our present-day giraffe. The predators included not only the saber-toothed tiger but also a type of a lion, leopard, and large hyena. Along with the animals, several types of early protohumans crept about. At first these creatures were vegetarians, but some later slowly developed into erect, prowling meat eaters. They used crude tools and fire. Now collectively known as the australopithecine, they may have been scavengers, competing with larger predators for the animals killed by the lions, tigers, and hyenas. It was the strange world of the Pleistocene, when mammals ruled eastern Africa and the predecessors of humankind were beginning an illustrious climb out of savagery and up to domination of the animal kingdom.

What made this particular donga in Tanzania famous was the discovery of several early hominids by the now well-known married anthropologists Louis and Mary Leakey. Their diggings in Olduvai in 1959–60 uncovered a famous australopithecine that rolled back human prehistory several million years.

The first australopithecine was not found here but in a limestone quarry in what is now Botswana, in 1924. The specimen was unearthed by Raymond Dart, an Australian-born anatomist (hence the name australopithecine) who was teaching in Johannesburg, South Africa. The find was an erect-walking creature with a brain larger than that of a chimpanzee but much more like a

contemporary human brain than that of a gorilla. Twelve years after the 1924 discovery, the skull of an adult female was uncovered by Dr. Broom, a physician and paleontologist; this form was called *Australopithecus africanus*. As the 1940s advanced, more skulls were found in Africa by Dart, Broom, and others.

The Leakey find in Olduvai in 1960 was part of a brain case and lower jaw of a similar *Australopithecus* form, found together with chipped stone tools, which the species undoubtedly used. They called the form *Homo habilis* ("handy man"). Later that same year they unearthed fragments of a more advanced form, *Homo erectus,* the first creature to use fire as a tool. Still later, Richard Leakey, son of the famed husband-wife team, discovered the remains of a much earlier type of hominid in the Lake Rudolph (now Lake Turkana) region of northern Kenya—fossil bones dated at 2.8 million years old! Olduvai, then, serves as a remarkable outdoor window on a world of long, long ago.

When one stands on the rim of Olduvai, looking across this site of early human occupation, with lone Thomson's gazelles here and there twitching their little tails to the sound of grunting, migrating wildebeest far out on the plains, a strange feeling of connection to antiquity arises. Here in the wilds of the African *veld* is where our distant relatives became *Homo sapiens* and slowly developed as human beings, in a valley not far from the grassy savannah that still teems with so much game. It is a place for deep reflection.

LAKE MANYARA NATIONAL PARK is situated perhaps a couple of hours' driving time from Olduvai, about seventy miles southwest of Arusha, Tanzania. While it is a small national park—only about 250 square miles—it possesses such a diversity of natural features that it can best be described as a naturalist's paradise in miniature.

Manyara is to the lover of plants and animals what Olduvai is to those interested in rocks and human origins. Moreover, exploring this gem of a place is not primarily to see the tree-climbing lions for which it is noted but also to view a microcosm of fascinating mammals, birds, and plants, to say nothing of the varied physiography. Manyara seems to offer many aspects of East Africa all rolled into one small package. Here a rugged slice of the high escarpment of the Great Rift Valley shows cool, freshwater rivulets and hot springs, plus a picturesque forest with an acacia woodland and several marshes. There are a number of savannahs and a bushveld filled with herds of game. Present also are several lakeshore lagoons, some modest sand rivers, and finally the alkaline lake by the same name.

Although a single day is hardly sufficient to do justice to this remarkable park, enough of a feel can be gained to whet one's appetite and make one want to return. Many tourists keep coming back to Manyara because it seems to embody so effectively all that one imagines wild Africa to be. Others return because they love to stay at Lake Manyara Lodge—a delightful, airy facility located on the escarpment, where the scenery is rich, the weather cool, and the bird viewing unsurpassed. Here even the tensest visitor can fully unwind and achieve relaxation.

The approach is by way of the small town of Mto wa Mhu, or Mosquito Creek. A stop in the village of Manyara is a welcome break. Its name comes from one of the smaller euphorbias from which the Masai make a living fence for their *manyattas,* or homesteads. Frequently other tour groups are already in the town. A dozen or so

vendors mind stalls full of goods on display, each owner most anxious to make some sales. They carry a variety of tourist items: wooden animal carvings, face masks, strings of colorful beads, elephant hair bracelets, mahogany letter openers, Masai spears, and crudely painted leather shields. One also sees fly whisks made of animal tails, ebony figurines and busts of Masai people, and woven baskets. Buyers play hard to get, haggle a lot, but finally make a deal, often for prices much lower than in the cities.

As we entered the park and began to roll slowly through the forest, a leopard suddenly sprang from a low tree and went sailing across the road ahead of our van, only to vanish in the bush. Then elephants begin crossing the brick-red dirt road. The driver halted as six huge pachyderms moved energetically ahead, probably bound for a lusher forest. Manyara is known to have far too many elephants for a small park, so efforts have been under way by noted naturalists, such as Ian Douglas Hamilton, to give the park corridors to additional forest habitats.

The unusual tree-climbing lions of Manyara are an astonishing sight. We saw only one lion in a tree, although the place is distinguished for this and it is known to be a fairly common occurrence. Just why these felines do this here (as also in Ruwenzori National Park in Uganda), no one knows for certain. It could be to get away from elephants or rhino, both of which may make sleeping on the ground uneasy for large cats. Others claim it is to gain a better view of passing prey animals. Still others believe lions climb to avoid safari ants, which can be particularly vicious in the wetter woodlands near the lake.

The total lion population in Manyara is not large, perhaps several prides at best. They feed mostly on impala, zebra, and Cape buffalo. In the open savannah one sees small herds of buffalo, all amply fed. About a thousand of these blackish bovines are present in the park, including at least 150 old, retired bulls.

The most popular viewing area for wildlife is the lakeshore habitat. This is a good place for groups to relax in their vehicle, eat a boxed lunch, and watch the activities of hippos in the pools, where they cavort in small groups all day long. They have plowed out a wide channel to the main lake but come to several lagoons to bathe in usual hippo fashion, always partially submerged and noisy. They rise and sink and snort, and seemingly yawn at every change of position. The indolent beasts bask in the water by day and come out in the evening to graze in the sedge-strewn marshes and grassy savannahs.

The lakeshore here is almost always lined with waterbirds: white- and pink-backed pelicans, Egyptian geese, ducks, coots, and various storks and herons. Where trees are present near the water, eight different kinds of kingfishers can be seen, flying about and frequently diving for fish. And of course the fish eagle also is common here, its calls of territorial assertion heard incessantly near the lakeshore. Hundreds of small birds can be seen flitting around picturesque palms and wild fig trees and in the savannah habitats. The serious birder can check off long lists of insectivorous and perching birds; some three hundred species are known to occur in the park.

Manyara has many confusing roads and lanes. To avoid backtracking and to see as much as possible in a short time, the services of a competent guide are well worth the extra expense. Usually local guides can be hired and picked up at the park gate.

In the afternoon, probably after seeing more

elephant, impala, and zebra, most groups proceed to a large clearing where numerous baboons can be seen feeding. Giraffes may look down at the primates from behind bordering tall acacias. The clearing is frequently alive with olive-backed baboons, sometimes as many as 250 in a single troop, their busy hands working in the grass. All are nervous feeders. Apparently several large groups converge here, yet no quarreling goes on. They are simply too busy picking up morsels of grass (mostly star grass), which they pluck away, first with one hand and then the other, glancing up momentarily, heads bobbing.

Before leaving Manyara (the park closes at 6:30 P.M.), our group was treated to a good view of Van der Decken's hornbills and, at one point, a pair of ground hornbills. They posed beautifully along the edge of a small savannah. Finally, as if all this wasn't enough for a delightful day, just outside the park, in lengthening golden shadows, a large herd of impala showed up. Mostly females, their red and white coats stood out noticeably in the fading sunlight. Herded gently from behind by a striking male with gorgeous lyre-shaped horns, the group glided slowly past us like a line of ballerinas dancing away, as if bidding us farewell from their marvelous paradise of Manyara.

NGORONGORO CRATER is another place one simply must see. Of all the meccas of the wild in Africa, this spectacular volcanic superbowl ringed by high cliffs surely ranks supreme as a gathering place for thousands of herbivores and their associated predatory followers—a seemingly self-contained eden, an ecosystem that strikes one as a world apart. Perhaps because of the dramatic impact of the physical setting, people who have visited often talk about it and long to return.

The approach to Ngorongoro makes one's first view of it memorable. The dirt road in winds across reddish low hills and areas of maize cultivation, followed by high grassland where Masai herdsmen still follow their cattle across treeless slopes. As you roll up toward higher and higher country, a different world comes into view: a zone of lush greenery and heavy bush is reached at about eight thousand feet—the high, forested rim of an old volcanic crater, one of several in Tanzania's crater highlands. Here Ngorongoro is king of them all—the largest and most impressive dormant crater on earth today and a place noted for its extraordinary animal life. The oval-shaped saucer is twelve miles long by ten miles wide. The interior depression, the caldera, drops some 2,500 feet below the rim, an awesome basin of some eighty thousand acres with a misty countenance and an eerie look from above. Seen from within, the crater is a nearly circular setting of rich, verdant vegetation. It is this vegetation that makes Ngorongoro the unique place that it is—and has been for thousands of years. The lush green growth, flourishing year in and year out, attracts the wildlife and, in many cases, holds it there.

The reason for the greenery is cooler temperatures and higher rainfall that is more consistent through the year. While the habitat is not tropical rain forest, sufficient rainfall occurs to keep the floor vegetation fresh and thriving. Some wildlife species, such as giraffe, elephant, buffalo, hyrax, and others, find the forested habitats to their liking; most herbivores prefer the grassland floor and remain there year-round. Some migrant grazers come down into the crater seasonally, entering the caldera when the pasturage outside on the plains is poor but leaving again when the plains green up. The predators, however—principally lion, cheetah, hyena, and leopard—find their Ngorongoro eden bountiful all year and seldom leave.

Masai tribesmen, too, find Ngorongoro much to their liking. They are a pastoral people, herding their cattle from place to place, but living harmoniously with the wildlife. Traditional use of the area for pasture is the main reason Ngorongoro is not classified as a national park but rather as a conservation area. Over the years the numbers of Masai in the crater have come to be tightly controlled, and at present no Masai manyattas are actually in the crater itself.

Most tourists going to Ngorongoro today stay only a night or two on the rim, just enough time to enjoy the cool, beautiful surroundings and to make one or two game runs down into the crater. There are only two places to stay up on the rim: a log lodge and a more modern one. Here the days are crisp and nights always cold enough to require heat in the rooms and plenty of bedcovers. In the late afternoon, before the sun dips behind the rim and the crater becomes enveloped in fog, one can walk around the log cabins of the Ngorongoro Crater Lodge (one of the oldest in Africa) and thoroughly enjoy the shrubs, lovely flowers, and views. Perched on a precipice near the lodge is a tree teahouse where one can enjoy a sundowner and gaze down into the great volcanic bowl where distant wildebeest and zebra look like beetles on a blue-green carpet.

On one of our trips to Africa, my wife and I stayed at this delightful old lodge and made a trip down into the crater. A couple from New York accompanied us on the game drive down into the caldera. Gangs of wildebeest and herds of zebra stared at us here and there, all completely unafraid. Several big eland wandered about. We saw

fig. 13. Ngorongoro black rhino with calf. The species is seriously on the decline all over eastern and central Africa.

the well-known white rhino dubbed Gertie, with her notably long front horn, and another rhino mother with her calf. At an alkaline lake, flamingos waded about, feeding, eyed intently from the shore by several hyenas. We spotted and photographed several lionesses in the tall grass and, later, visited a Masai manyatta.

On our way out, going up the crater's jagged walls, our driver put the Land Rover in four-wheel drive to negotiate a route so steep and treacherous that we thought the motor would burn out. Near the crest of the rim we stopped to let a herd of buffalo cross before us. These big bovine creatures need to be given a wide berth for they can crush or tip over a vehicle. An angry or even an uneasy buffalo can be a formidable proposition.

That evening at the lodge we had a delightful dinner. We were served zebra steak, delicious, but so tough that my front tooth got chipped on it. It was Christmas Eve, with a decorated cedar tree and a music box playing carols. Our New York friends were on their honeymoon and so were we. We stayed for a while following dinner to enjoy some drinks, but decided to leave early to beat the fog. So we said good night to our companions and retired from the dining room, hoping to walk the 200 yards to our cabin in reasonable visibility.

Just outside the lodge a Masai guard with a long spear met us. "I take you, your cabin, yes?" he asked. "You know, big animals around." Thinking this was a considerate gesture and a chance for him to make a shilling, we agreed.

Walking briskly in the night's chilly blackness, with the guard's torchlight pointing the way, we encountered wisps of fog already wafting across the crater rim. Then ten yards from our cabin the guard suddenly halted. "See—there," he whispered. "Buffalo. Quick! Hurry! Go in and no open door." We did and the man disappeared so fast that we had no chance to tip him. We planned to do that the next morning.

Before turning on the oil lamp in the cabin, we quietly felt our way with a flashlight to the bathroom. There through the open window we could faintly see six buffalo grazing in front of the other couple's cabin. The sight was worrisome. What if our friends suddenly decided to leave the lodge and had no guard, and then found themselves before the dangerous beasts? There was no phone and no way to get word to them. We could only hope that these buffalo were peaceable. One thing was certain: hunting had long been a vague memory in Ngorongoro. Much of the game we had seen appeared accepting of a human presence among them. After taking a flash photo of the buffalo from the open window, it was time to turn on the gas heat and retire.

Next morning at breakfast our friends seemed hardly perturbed and certainly unscathed.

"Did the Masai guard escort you last night?" my wife inquired curiously.

"What guard?" came a quick reply.

"Well, did you see the buffalo?"

The bride's eyes opened wide. "What buffalo?" she shot back. Apparently the big fellows had moved out soon after we retired.

More than a decade later we returned to Ngorongoro, this time in a safari group of ten, and booked at the newer, more sophisticated Ngorongoro Wildlife Lodge, also strategically perched on the rim of the crater. Arriving in time for lunch, we arranged for a game run down into the crater

in the afternoon. Using two four-wheel-drive Land Rovers, we made the treacherous descent in nervous silence but in good order.

Once on the crater floor we were immediately treated to a parade of wildebeest, zebra, and Grant's and Thomson's gazelle. Several groups of hyenas appeared and a herd of buffalo wandered in the distance. We looked hard for eland but saw only one. The Masai manyatta we had visited was gone and so was Gertie; she had been poached some years earlier. Rolling slowly across the grassy savannah, our driver led us to two lionesses. They seemed well fed and were ambling along toward an alkaline lake, possibly for an evening's drink of water. We did not follow them although the temptation to do so was great. Some seventy lions are said to be permanent residents of the crater. The herbivore population is put at between twenty-five and thirty-five thousand.

Suddenly we spotted two cheetahs standing beautifully poised in the fading sunlight, eyeing a small herd of wildebeest. In hushed voices we asked our driver to stay close to them. They began a slow stalk. Both of our vehicles eased along, one slightly behind the other but moving up. "I believe they're going to make a chase," one man said. And he was right. The two lithe bodies suddenly lunged forward into a furious sprint, picking up great speed (they are capable of close to seventy miles per hour), and headed right for the wildebeest. Soon one cheetah grabbed a wildebeest by the throat and together predator and prey reared up high into the air, quivered for a moment, then fell to earth, the wildebeest gasping. In a flash the other cheetah sailed in for a back hold. In less than a minute the wildebeest moaned its last.

Now four big dark cheetah eyes glared at us,

fig. 14. *A common cheetah* (left) *in contrast to the rare king cheetah. Courtesy South African Tourism Board*

their jaws holding flesh. We had halted only 75 feet from them and witnessed and photographed the whole dramatic episode. No one spoke. Our hearts pounded over our first sighting of a kill in Africa. But the action was not over.

Suddenly five chuckling hyenas raced to the scene. One aggressive hyena lunged toward the cheetahs but was driven off by one of them, which momentarily left the kill. Meanwhile the other four robbers charged in and chased the other cheetah off. Instantly all five hyenas tore away at the wildebeest, while the cheetahs, exhausted and overpowered, slowly withdrew. There would be no more hunts for them this evening. Tomorrow, perhaps, in daylight, but seldom after dark. It would be a dinnerless night for two cheetahs in Ngorongoro Crater.

Not so for the hyenas. Wildly giggling, tearing away first at the paunch then at whatever was nearest, they devoured the stolen carcass in ten minutes. Watching the noisy melee, it was difficult not to feel antipathy toward the hyenas and sympathy for the cheetahs. But the hyenas, no doubt, also had young mouths to feed at their burrows.

With the sun now well below the crater rim and darkness fast approaching, we slowly turned out of the great grassland and began our long drive across the crater floor and then up the volcanic wall. Again we spoke little, feeling drained of emotional energy. It was a while before someone's remark broke the spell of our encounter with life primeval and returned us to the more mundane—contemplating a scotch and soda to settle our minds.

Most visitors, when departing the famous volcanic crater, find it fitting to stop at the grave of Bernard Grzimek who, with his noted zoologist father, did so much to help publicize the Serengeti and Ngorongoro. Bernard died when the small plane he was piloting crashed into the crater wall. A simple granite tombstone next to the road marks his resting place. The Grzimeks authored the acclaimed *Serengeti Shall Not Die* (1960). Leaving the site, one is compelled to wonder about the optimism of this father–son team of conservationists. Should their hopes and dreams not fail them—should the world indeed arrive at global environmental consciousness—the eden that is the Serengeti-Ngorongoro pride of wild East Africa will continue to thrive.

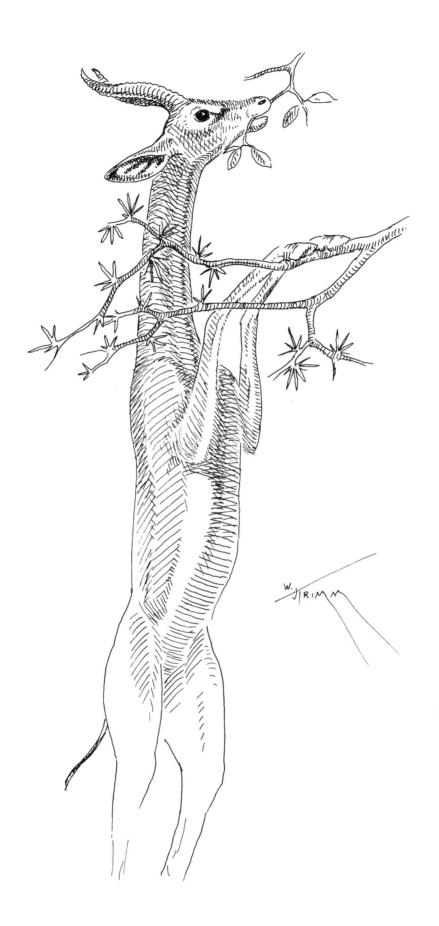

CHAPTER 7

The Marvels of Samburu and Meru

Two wildlife edens in Kenya's northern Great Rift Valley deserve mention in any book covering the premier game areas of East Africa. In these areas farther north are species one does not see in the parks already mentioned; these places offer some degree of departure from the main tourist circuit because their attractions are more rarefied. They may not have the between-the-eyes force of embodying "Africa" as do Serengeti or Ngorongoro and cannot substitute for those, but they can complement them. One is the ever-popular Buffalo Springs National Reserve–Samburu National Park, some 214 miles north of Nairobi, and the other is Meru National Park, a less frequented but appealing park located on the lower eastern slope of Mount Kenya. Most tour agencies shun Meru because the roads and facilities there are less developed.

The drive to BUFFALO SPRINGS NATIONAL RESERVE–SAMBURU NATIONAL PARK passes through some of the wildest, most picturesque country in East Africa. Although one is still a hundred fifty miles away from the northern border here, this area was once called the Northern Frontier District. There are stunning views of stately Mount Kenya, forest-draped high escarpments, deep valleys, and faraway dry river scrublands. As one nears the reserve, the road gets lonelier, bumpier, and dustier. On occasions a driver may even appear lost, for there are few road signs. This points up a reason why it can be unwise to roam around in wild country on one's own in a rented car. In remote areas petrol stations are few and far between. Moreover, should a breakdown occur, help is not readily available. With a tour group, one has more peace of mind. (Among the things that may make the northern frontier experience memorable are Pokot tribesmen suddenly accosting one, spear in hand; but their purpose is mostly to beg cigarettes or to sell wares.)

The elephants of Buffalo Springs–Samburu are a special attraction. Usually one runs into them long before reaching the reserve gate and the *rondavels* (circular thatched chalets) of Buffalo Springs. At Buffalo Springs the behemoths often plow in single file right through the scant bush, producing a cloud of dust as they make their way to the permanent river called the Ewaso Ng'iro coming out of the Aberdare highlands. Samburu Game Lodge itself is located some ten miles farther on the bank of the river. Around the comfortable facility lies a distinctive world. At the lodge, where more greenery is present, the trumpeting of unseen elephants is more than subliminal music to the visiting guests. At times elephants may swim the river to the bank where the lodge is and proceed through the grounds, sending surprised guests dashing for their tents. A flimsy canvas tent is obviously no protection from a fast-plodding elephant, but because tents generally represent shelter for people, elephants seldom bother them.

Elephant watching from a quiet minibus is preferable, if less exciting. Relaxed and still, one can get a real feeling for an elephant family going about their daily business, human visitors notwithstanding. Usually led by a large matriarch, who takes full charge of all goings-on, a family group on the riverbank can be a scene of jumbo dimensions: huge animals consorting, some squirting water on themselves and one another, a few pushing and shoving gently, others drinking, bathing, and even, it seems, snorkeling. The calves look vulnerable in among the giant, ponderous legs of adults, but the babies are seldom stepped on. After much drinking and bathing, next begins the mud-splashing ritual. One wonders why elephants go through so much effort to wash and bathe, only to plaster themselves afterward with gooey mud. Perhaps it's one way of scraping vermin off their thick hides, maybe it's because the mud has a cooling effect on the skin after baking in the sun, or maybe it's protection against the sun and biting insects. The frolicking of elephants on the river can continue for an hour or more before the

matriarch issues a signal for all to depart. And when thirty, forty, or more elephants finally leave the river in single file, their great backs glistening in the evening sunlight, it is a picture long to be remembered.

A second special sight of Samburu is the distinctive antelope called the gerenuk. This slender, rather large gazelle with an exceptionally elongated neck has the startling habit of standing on its hind legs and stretching upward to browse from tree limbs. Sometimes holding this awkward looking position for a long time, this dandy of the semiarid scrub is a photographer's dream. Eons of such body straining have given the antelope its special features, plus a name which in Somali means "giraffe-necked antelope." Another name given it is giraffe-gazelle. Although this 80- to 115-pound gazelle occurs elsewhere, notably in Somalia and Ethiopia, it can best be seen in East Africa in Samburu National Park.

Gerenuks travel in small groups of seven or eight and, like impala, always seems to be herded by a regal, stately horned male; the females do not have horns. Being a browser, this agile antelope often use a foreleg to pull down a tree branch. They eat the limbs cleanly while standing outstretched, their delicate white bellies showing prominently, even from far away. According to authorities, these ruddy-brown gazelles are among the few antelope in Africa that have been extending their range appreciably over the past sixty years, indicating that they are a highly adaptive species.

Also seen in similar, but usually drier, bush habitat as the gerenuk is another marvel, the beautiful beisa oryx. This magnificent and robust antelope has long, straight horns and striking coloration. Its smoky gray body color is accented with white underparts and lines of black and white on the face and belly. Beisa oryx move about unhurriedly, usually in bands of six to ten but at times in herds of up to sixty. The male weighs up to 450 pounds. Both male and female have long, stiletto-like horns; thus the animal is a challenge for any predator; even lions have been known to be impaled on them. The oryx defends itself with its head held low, a stance menacing to any foe, large or small. The animals hold well for photographers and are worth considerable effort to see. And because the oryx is a species of the dry northeasterly part, many visitors to Africa do not see them.

Samburu is also one of the few places in Kenya where the visitor is privileged to see two kinds of zebra: the common Burchell's with its large, broad stripes and the rarer Grevy's zebra with its shorter, more delicate, narrower markings. An individual's stripes are each a bit different in both species. The ranges of the two overlap here, although their habitat in the main is quite different. The Burchell's is primarily a grassland dweller, while its narrow-striped, handsomer cousin is more apt to favor arid brushlands and semidesert steppes.

To see these two well-groomed, plump, horse-like creatures side by side is a rare event and a sight that can be quite poignant, especially when you least expect it. Once in Samburu I was watching a herd of Burchell's zebra with a Kikuyu driver named Omari, who spoke English and Swahili and was normally calm and composed, when he suddenly announced, "Oh, Bwanas, look— *pundamilia,* the very narrow striped donkey!" A Grevy's zebra had come into view, and what a refreshing sight it was for eyes strained by hours of scanning for animals in the bright sunlight.

The warthog of the scrublands is a diverting creature to watch in Samburu. For some reason

the warthogs here appear to be less skittish than those elsewhere. The small hoglike animals occur from the Horn of Africa in a wide belt all the way to the West African coast and south as far as eastern South Africa. They inhabit the Kalahari Desert and range from there westward into Namibia and Angola. Perhaps their less suspicious nature in Buffalo Springs–Samburu is due to the presence of lots of protective cover: low, heavy thornbush thickets, tall riverine grasses, and many aardvark burrows in which they can take quick refuge. Also few vehicles disturb them here. When fleeing from danger, mostly from a lion or leopard, a warthog may scurry backward into a hole so as to be able to use its tusks for defense. On the open plains, where protective cover is not readily available, the creatures appear more nervous and are seemingly always on the run. Good photos of running warthogs are difficult to get, and even faraway still shots can be disappointing. But in Samburu the picture-taking success ratio is high. Here one can get excellent shots of warthogs.

On one game run in Buffalo Springs we watched several warthog families for a long time. In each case they were most accommodating. With our minibus parked and motor turned off, we watched and photographed them from the open roof hatch and obtained some fine shots. Twice we saw several members grazing while down on their horny, densely haired "knees"—a delightful pose to observe.

Another creature for which Samburu is noted to provide privileged viewing is the Nile crocodile, a species fast disappearing all over Africa. Millions of crocodiles once inhabited the wild rivers and lakes of the continent. Samuel Baker and his wife, while making a trip up the Nile, saw thousands of the reptiles. Around Lake Albert and Murchison Falls (in what is now Uganda) they had close encounters with them. But today, habitat destruction, wanton killing, and poaching have drastically reduced their range outside formally protected areas. The Nile crocodile is now said to be scarce in the lower Nile (Sudan and Egypt) but found in limited numbers in the upper Nile, including its tributaries and lakes. Fortunately, however, there are wild places, mostly in preserves and parks, where these interesting creatures can still be seen and safely watched. The Ewaso Ng'iro in Samburu is one such place.

Time was when the usual feeling among explorers, hunters, and casual observers was that the African crocodile was a hideous leftover from a time millions of years ago, a mean, repulsive, dangerous creature that could never be trusted. The conventional wisdom was that anyone coming close to a crocodile asleep on a sand bar or lolling in the water would soon be turned into mincemeat if not careful. Masses of crocodiles on a riverbank would be especially dangerous (as Tarzan films graphically showed)—a menace too formidable even to contemplate.

Today we know better. Studies have helped us understand that, while these animals are certainly efficient predators, they are also of interest for some remarkable social dynamics and for parental protection of the young. For instance, Nile crocodiles have been found to hunt cooperatively and to divide the spoils. Breeding adults are monogamous, at least seasonally, and guard their offspring by means of a complex system of social behavior. Crocs seen picking up their young are not necessarily displaying cannibalism but may, in fact, be transporting their babies safely from high ground to the river.

Crocodile watching can be fun. At Samburu one can take an early afternoon tour to a croc lookout, going by van to a river viewpoint. If there are not already crocodiles present and basking, one may see them emerge from the swift current, water flowing from their backs, to lumber up onto a wet slide, exposing a length of perhaps thirteen feet. Ashore, the creatures drop to their bellies and rest, often hardly twenty feet from startled onlookers. A crude barrier separates the people from the reptiles. We watched one croc rise and lumber farther forward, stopping only 6 feet from the fence to settle down again and open its cavernous orange mouth. It was enough to make everyone jump. But the protective fence is sufficient to allow viewers a margin of safety. At such moments some observers become breathless and not a few feel chills race along the spine. Gazing into those eyes, that terrible gaping mouth with rows of huge teeth, one may have difficulty escaping an impression of malevolence. It is exciting to see a living relic from long ago—a species perhaps as old as sixty-five million years, its antecedents going back two hundred million years to the time when the crocodilians first appeared on earth. Yet the crocodile in Samburu is no fossil, no museum piece; it's the real thing.

Some onlookers back off, preferring to watch the reptile from a safe distance. For today's observers to realize that here crocodiles have survived for so many millennia and thrived so successfully—and that we can still see them virtually unchanged—is enough to give one a feeling of wonder and admiration. And one can extend viewing into the evening: at Samburu Game Lodge there is an open, walled-in terrace where croc watching under the floodlights is popular. Every evening at sundown one or more of the

Ewaso Ng'iro's hefty marvels come out of the river to feed on bones dumped onto the sand by the kitchen help. When the crocs arrive, a measure of excitement runs through the place, visitors heading to the terrace for the ritual.

The Nile crocodile is the largest and most common of three crocodilians found in Africa. It can weigh up to eighteen hundred pounds and reach a length of eighteen feet. Buoyant in water, it is a powerful swimmer. On land, despite its bulk and lumbering appearance, it can lunge forward for thirty or forty yards at a pace faster than a man can run. The normal foods of these reptiles are fish, turtles, snakes, and unsuspecting birds and mammals, not people. While each year the fifty thousand or so crocodiles still found in Africa take a certain number of human lives, the incidence of systematic man-eating is rare. Crocs also feed on dead, mostly drowned animals, and when the great migratory animal herds cross rivers, as on the Mara, the crocs have a sumptuous feast. Their characteristic twisting action when feeding is a means of wringing chunks of flesh off a carcass, after which they gulp down food. Crocs cannot chew their food and so must swallow it in chunks.

But they suffer when food is scarce. After the long rains of spring have ended and the rivers begin to lose their flow and dry up, crocs try to find safety in ooze and mud. The bullfrogs and lungfish have long slithered deeper into their subterranean hideouts and are no longer available as food for the reptiles. The crocs often go without food for a long time, even all summer, but their rugged hides must be kept moist lest the searing sun dehydrate them. Then when the rivers are up, crocs can again be seen. The survival of the crocodiles in Samburu, as is the case everywhere in Africa, is linked to human attitudes toward them.

These relics can survive if people will it so.

Samburu National Park often has other surprises in store for visitors. One day as a small group of us rolled along a sandy lane in dry habitat, our driver spotted something unusual in the faraway trackless bush. All eyes soon were glued to the spot. Several eager beavers wanted to drive nearer, but our leader decreed this risky. We could easily get a flat tire from the thornbush all around and be left stranded. Besides, the rule was not to leave the track in this wild country. But the sudden desire to see something special was so great that our leader was quickly overruled. Soon we went into the bush, bouncing, swaying back and forth, plowing forward like a bulldozer on a spree. Then we saw them: a pack of wild dogs, or Cape hunting dogs, on a fresh kill. What luck! We all went to the windows and roof hatch. Large-eared canines splotched with tan, black, and white, they paid us little attention as our vehicle rolled in, stopping within 30 feet of them. Although the animals were somewhat obscured by brush, we did get some fair views and pictures of the dogs in action. We stayed for at least twenty minutes and then slowly backed off, the dogs still feasting. It was for many a first experience with wild dogs and, in a way, everyone was glad we broke the rule. What a thrill this sighting was, precisely because these animals are now so rare.

Samburu and Buffalo Springs are both especially noted for their colorful birds and lovely bird songs, besides the large mammal species. Bird enthusiasts coming here report seeing hundreds of species in a single day, ranging from such large forms as the ostrich, secretary bird, and the ground hornbill to hawks, ducks, herons, eagles, and vultures, plus a host of small and beautiful passerines. Rollers, weavers, sunbirds, and kingfishers are common around the lodges. One is never out of hearing of the cooing of doves and the delicate voices of lovebirds. Like the lakes of the Great Rift Valley, the Buffalo Springs–Samburu country is an ornithologist's paradise.

MERU NATIONAL PARK, in contrast to Buffalo Springs–Samburu, is a much more heavily forested area. One reason to visit it is that, this being a smaller park and not heavily patronized, those who do go there may find they have the place pretty much to themselves. Second, Meru has several distinct habitat types and plenty of wildlife. Species readily seen here and sometimes harder to find elsewhere include the interesting birds called the honeyguide and hamerkop; the solitary master hunter of the scrub, the leopard; and the big white rhino. Each alone is worth a trip to Meru to see.

If one were to fly over Meru, four distinct habitats could be seen. On the eastern slopes of Mount Kenya, at eight thousand feet, sprawls a montane rain forest zone. Below this is heavy scrubland, which continues down to the five-thousand-foot level. Still lower, where rainfall is scarcer, lies savannah country, open terrain with plenty of grass cover and some sparse woodlands. Finally there is the lowland riverine habitat of the Tana River, Kenya's largest river system, which traverses some of the wildest country in Africa.

Although the park is not large, its mixed terrain, varied vegetation, and limited roads make Meru a wonderful wildlife refuge and a park deserving more recognition than is usually accorded it.

Meru teems with bird life, particularly game birds, waterbirds, weavers, sunbirds, and warblers. This extraordinary abundance of birds is due to

the richness of the Tana River plain. The habitat twists and turns for several hundred miles, finally merging with the coastal lowlands of the Indian Ocean. Draining into the Tana are several small tributaries and dozens of intermittent streams; this area also holds marshes and many water holes. During the dry season most of the wetlands hold only ooze. Here the turtles and frogs bury themselves deep in the mud, to emerge again when the rains come. Meru's location on this major riparian corridor is the key to its wealth of bird life. While the park is limited in area—although larger than Samburu—much of the wildlife moves freely in and out of the park to satisfy food, water, and territorial requirements.

The overall Meru-Samburu region is the country made famous by Joy Adamson in Born Free, chronicling the life of the orphaned lion cub, Elsa. The story of how she was cared for, reared, and eventually returned to the wild was also made into a successful film. Joy Adamson, who loved animals and Meru, was killed in the area not long ago but her dedicated work with lions lives on, as does the great conservation work of her late husband, George Adamson, killed more recently by poachers.

One cannot write about Meru and Born Free without digressing to cite a story told to me about a woman in Nairobi who went to see the film when it was playing there. It seems she entered the darkened theater a bit late and carefully felt her way into a center seat. When her eyes became adjusted to the dim light, she noticed with surprise that the woman in the seat in front of her was accompanied by a lioness in the adjoining seat, the animal quietly watching the movie. After getting up her nerve, she tapped the woman in front on the shoulder and inquired quietly,

fig. 15. The endangered wild dog, or Cape hunting dog, is considered an efficient predator.

"Tell me, please, is your lioness enjoying the film?" The lioness owner turned to reply, "I really don't know, my dear, but she sure enjoyed the book."

Of the bird marvels of Meru, the hamerkop (meaning "hammer head") and honeyguide are especially noteworthy. Both have interesting habits, the former quite baffling, the second of some economic value to local people, who seek out the bird's services.

The hamerkop, belonging to the same order as storks, herons, and ibises, frequents the banks of the Tana and its tributaries and is absolutely fascinating to watch. Measuring about twenty inches in length, it has an overall brown color and a head indeed shaped rather like a hammer. The bird has a dignified air but is noisy, even downright raucous, uttering harsh cries both when feeding and upon being startled into a sudden takeoff. Often hamerkops are seen in pairs or in groups of up to seven, seemingly always looking for amphibians in the marshes and water holes. The female hamerkop, the same dull brown as the male, lays from three to six eggs, which hatch in thirty days. The nestlings remain in the nest for about fifty days and are fed by both parents.

The distinctive things about these birds are their bizarre nest-building habits and their incredible jumping activities. When breeding, the birds construct some of the largest, most amazing nests in the bird world, exceeded in size and weight only by those of eagles. Hamerkop nests are built close to water out of huge assemblages of branches, sticks, reeds, grasses, and mud. One nest in Meru measured five feet across, although it contained a center nesting hole just twelve inches in diameter. The birds are serious avian engineers, taking up to six busy weeks to build a new nest or to add substantially to an old one.

During this period they seem to be the busiest birds in Africa—and also the jumpiest. The jumping of hamerkops, so far as is known, is a performance unique in the bird world. One bird stands on the back of its mate and begins a joyous jumping act, up and down, up and down, perhaps as many as fifty times. Then the partners trade places and the tireless jumping resumes. Again and again the birds go through this strange act. No one knows why they do it—it is just another avian mystery that may never be solved by bird-watchers.

Honeyguides are small passerine birds that inhabit the scrub country and grassy savannah. They too are avian marvels. While several species of honeyguides are known to lead people to the hives of honeybees, the black-throated honeyguide (yellowish on the back and white on the breast) is particularly noted for guiding honey hunters to bee trees. Such a hunter imitates the call of the honeyguide and, receiving an answering "ke, ke, ke, ke, ke, ke, ke, ke," follows it, sometimes for long distances. By tradition, the hunter, thus guided, upon finally getting to the bee tree and robbing the bees of their honey (often getting badly stung in the process despite the use of smoke to befuddle the bees), offers the bird a reward: enough honeycomb and honey around for the honeyguide to eat its fill.

Honeyguides also have traits less appealing in the human frame of reference than their guiding behavior, however. They are what ornithologists call brood parasites—that is, they lay their eggs in the nests of other birds for the incubation and feeding of their young. Roger Tory Peterson says it is probable that the fourteen members of the honeyguide family (all but one of which are found in Africa) are brood parasites of hole-nesting birds like the barbets, woodpeckers, and starlings. Clearly this practice of raising different species within a brood must be a confusing state of affairs for the surrogate parents.

While game at Meru cannot compare with that on the seething Serengeti plains, this park does harbor many of the same species. The problem is that the game cannot be seen as readily here because of the heavier, concealing cover. Elephants are present, as are other members of the big five. Lions are often seen singly, as are leopards, which seem more at home in the thorn scrub than out on the plains. Buffalo are quite common and are often seen all over the Meru bush. They are among the few big game members that are widespread in Africa and appear to be holding their own. Here in Meru, these large bovine animals can be quite dangerous, especially when surprised by someone walking about in the bush. Thus one is better off to stay in a vehicle or close to it. However, special permission can be obtained to go out on a foot safari and even to set up a campsite in an approved area. A friend and colleague of mine who once chose to pitch his own tent in the bush reported having lions around him all night long, scaring him badly.

Giraffes are very much at home in Meru because of the abundance of trees. On each of several game drives we were able to catch some remarkable glimpses of them feeding. At one point we also came upon a dead, disemboweled giraffe, a body so bloated and full of flies that we had to leave without ascertaining what had killed it; probably lions were responsible, the only predators capable of pulling down such a large animal.

Among the antelope, the lesser kudu is commonly spotted, but the animals are shy and forever hiding their lovely twisted horns in the foliage of trees and bushes. The Grevy's zebra is present, as is the ungainly wildebeest. In one game run in central Meru we saw many wildebeest that had apparently died from hoof and mouth disease or anthrax. These deadly diseases hit many herbivores but it was the first time we had seen so many dead of one species in one place.

The yellow baboon is frequently to be seen here, scurrying around acacia groves not far from water and frequently feeding on the ground. These baboons enjoy swinging up into in fig trees and are extremely fond of the fruit, often carrying morsels to the water's edge where they sometimes wash it before commencing to eat. Baboons are highly sociable, territorial in habit, and terribly nervous, which makes them difficult to photograph. They can also be dangerous if confronted. Looking a male straight in the eye is reputed to signify a challenge and could invite attack.

Tourists are routinely fascinated by baboons, and drivers of vehicles always stop when these creatures are around. On one trip, our group enjoyed the antics of a male being annoyed by an apparently frustrated female. The pair were together on a tree limb over a pool. While baboons have more than one mate, the males do try to confine their services to the females in one troop. At any rate, this particular male seemed disinterested and kept looking around, nonchalantly, as

the red-rumped female kept bothering him. Finally, in desperation, she rubbed her hind parts right into his and screamed. This was impudence at its highest. The big male swatted her rigorously across the neck, knocking her off the perch and into the water, screeching.

Meru has a limited number of lions; the most prominent big cat is the leopard. Although not often seen because of its nocturnal habits, leopards are much in evidence when one reads the tracks, which are everywhere, in dusty road ruts, around the sandy bases of termite mounds, along riverbanks and muddy water holes. Park rangers who make regular patrols toward evening report the sounds of hissing, snarling leopards as "very common." It is then that the large, solitary cats begin their serious hunting forays, pouncing on anything from a small hyrax to a Grant's gazelle. A leopard can dispatch an antelope twice its own body weight and then drag the carcass a long way to a convenient tree where, perhaps after one or more tries, it succeeds in getting its prey aloft and finally wedging it safely in a crotch, beyond the reach of bothersome lions and hyenas. To watch a 140-pound leopard carry a 140- or 160-pound antelope up a tree is to witness a Meru marvel performing an astonishing feat. A leopard is all muscle and, pound for pound, is stronger than a lion or any other wild cat. Little wonder that the leopard is faring quite well over Africa, where it is still widely distributed. In East Africa, Meru National Park remains one of its strongholds.

The leopard is a loner except briefly during mating time. Unlike the lion or cheetah, it lives alone, hunts alone, kills alone. While leopards do hunt in daylight, they prefer twilight and the long hours of night to do their stalking and killing. Cunning and stealth are their weapons. To witness a leopard making a kill is a rarity indeed. Most filmmakers cannot afford the long wait that it takes to film this lone predator making a daylight kill (although it has been done), and so often resort to captive leopards performing a coup de grace in compound situations. In Meru, perhaps one hundred leopards still roam the bushveld habitats.

The most outstanding marvel of Meru, however, is the rhinoceros. Both the black or hook-lipped and the white or square-lipped rhino are found here, surviving in the wild as seriously threatened species. They are the same gray in color but their differing lip structures reflect the black rhino being browsers and the white rhino grazers. The white rhino was nearly destroyed, continentwide; the southern white rhino in recent years has begun to increase again in southern Africa. More recently, poaching has drastically reduced the black rhino. Of the three, the northern white rhino is the most seriously endangered; just a handful remain in Kenya and Zaire. That makes the Meru rhino very special. During my most recent visit to Meru the total population of white rhinos in the park had been reduced to a protected group of six adults and one calf.

The white rhino is paradoxical in appearance; this bulky creature appears dignified, poised, and

fig. 16. Leopard on a monkey kill. Baboons are its favorite prey. Courtesy South African Tourism Board

fig. 17. One of several white rhinos surviving in Meru National Park.

even dainty on its three-toed feet. The small band we saw seemed healthy enough and roamed freely under tight protection—all munching on bushes and tearing away tall grass. White rhino are generally more docile than black rhino and are less readily aroused to charge. But one never knows. We watched them for a long time from beside our minibus, hoping against hope that one of the armed guards would invite us to come over and have a closer look. At last a come-hither signal came. Camera in hand, I advanced toward the guard and his charges. Soon we were eyeball to eyeball with the largest rhino bull. To me it felt momentous, made my heart pound, to be so close to an animal so large and so drastically endangered. The huge bull kept feeding away and never batted an eye.

The saga of the rhino is one of the saddest chapters in the history of the animal kingdom, a shameful commentary on the character of humankind in both Africa and Asia. The problem arises out of the belief that powdered rhino horn is a powerful medicine and that it also contains aphrodisiacal qualities, including cure of impotence in men. This contention has absolutely no basis in medical fact. Yet the myth persists and the clandestine traffic in rhino horn, mostly in Africa, continues. Several decades ago a six-pound rhino horn would bring as much as several hundred dollars. Today, because of scarcity and new heavy demands coming out of Yemen, the prices have shot up into the thousands of dollars. An investigation into illegal horn trafficking by an American living in Kenya, Esmond B. Martin (as reported in the *New York Times,* June 29, 1982), disclosed that some 60 percent of rhino horns were still sent to the Orient, mostly China, Korea, and Japan, but that around 40 percent went to Yemen, where the horn is used to decorate the handles of ceremonial daggers, called *djambia,* worn as a token of manhood. Before the oil boom, Yemen, a south Arabian country, was poor, but now, with wages high because of oil production, the decorative djambia are more easily afforded by young men. So the pressure on the rhino in Africa continues and poaching flourishes despite the best efforts of the authorities in Kenya and other African countries to stop it.

The abominable practice of poaching involves the use of all kinds of cruel devices: cable snares, pits, poison, spears, bows and arrows, and sometimes guns. As is typical in such black market situations, sometimes a guard can be bribed, for he can get a year's wages for allowing a single rhino to be killed. Some of the killings, especially by snares, involve hours, days, of terrible suffering, the animals slowly dying from thirst, exhaustion, and festered wounds. Often the sores become gangrenous and are besieged by maggots and ants.

At the time of this survey there were about fifteen thousand black rhinos in the wild in Africa and about three thousand white rhinos. In Uganda, Tanzania, and Kenya the rhino population in re-

cent years has dropped a devastating 90 percent.

The story of rhino decline is similar in Asia, where the feeling among conservationists is that, if the rhino disappears in Africa, it will likewise go in Asia. In the Orient there are three surviving main species: the Indian, Javan, and Sumatran, all badly reduced in numbers. Today the future of all rhino remains in doubt. The International Union for the Conservation of Nature, a worldwide conservation body headquartered in Switzerland, at one time estimated that there were only 1,135 one-horned Indian rhinos, 45 to 54 Javan, and perhaps only a few hundred Sumatran left. The largest concentration of the one-horned Indian rhinos seems to be in the jungles of Nepal's Chitwan National Park where, in October, 1983, only some three hundred remained. Riding atop tame Indian elephants on forays through twenty-five-foot high riverine grass, our safari encountered only one rhino. But because the grass was high and concealment good, it is entirely possible we may have missed several.

The park, three hundred square miles in size, is inhabited by some thirty-five breeding tigers, perhaps fifteen more cubs, and possibly another fifteen adults that wander in and out of the sanctuary. But the huge striped cats are not commonly seen; it is rhino searching and photographing from atop elephants that is most popular. While the tiger and the rhino in Nepal are the prime animals being given protection, a whole battalion of soldiers (some six hundred men) is now required to be on duty to protect the park's big animals.

There are those who feel, regrettably and sadly, that when it comes to protecting the wild rhino with armed rangers in Africa, or with a whole battalion of soldiers in one small park in Asia, we might as well acknowledge that we have lost the rhino. Others are not quite so pessimistic, citing as factors that may yet help us save rhinos from extinction newer and better forms of protection and management, widely scattered gene pools, forceful diplomatic efforts around the world to root out the illicit trade in rhino horn, and education of people concerned.

One thing seems clear: We have to try. It is hard enough to accept extinctions when they are accidents of habitat destruction and ignorance, but knowingly to permit the rhinos of the world to be eliminated for reasons of commerce is entirely unacceptable. We left the white rhinos of Meru reluctantly, our close encounter having made us more than ever conscious of the precariousness of their position.

CHAPTER 8

Approaching the Mountains of the Moon

As the high-soaring crowned eagle flies from Mount Elgon across Lake Victoria to the snow-covered Mountains of the Moon, it peers down upon one of the most verdant lands in eastern and central Africa: Uganda. The region has copious rainfall, much bright sunlight, rich red soils with thousands of intriguing termite mounds, numerous rivers and lakes, and highlands and lowlands; there are several national parks, coffee, tea, and banana plantations, and many towns and villages with interesting people and a remarkable history. Unfortunately the country has been beset by much poverty, strife, and political instability. From a natural history perspective, however, it was for centuries known as the "Pearl of Africa."

While Mount Elgon lies in westernmost Kenya, geographically and ecologically it falls within the Uganda equatorial ecosystem. Most visitors to Mount Elgon come from Kampala, Uganda's quaint capital city, because this mountain park is close to the city and a great place for hiking and cooling off. The park encompasses only the up-

per heights of the mountain, with headquarters in a one-time English governor's mansion. Visitors must be accompanied by an armed ranger as elephants and Cape buffalo are frequently encountered. The mountain rises to well over thirteen thousand feet above sea level but its four-mile-wide extinct volcanic crater is almost never seen on account of the clouds, mist, and fog. The lower slopes are a belt of greenery dominated by many magnificent *Podocarpus* trees.

The main attraction at Elgon is a huge limestone cavern called Kitum Cave, an undeveloped marvel of nature where herds of elephants come late in the afternoon to lick the limestone salts and siphon spring water from various water holes; here, too, perhaps as many as a million fruit bats cling to the ceilings at night. The bats pour out of the cave at daylight and return in the evening, often as the last of the elephants enter the cavern. With the aid of a strong torchlight one can explore the cave for hundreds of yards, slipping and sliding over great mounds of bat guano. In some passages the mounds are as large as houses. There are no maps of the cave and one can easily wander off and get lost. The only way out would be to follow the trumpeting sounds of elephants at the cave entrance late in the afternoon. Around the cave mouth are massive boulders and a rocky promontory. Any photographer or sound recordist taking up a post just before the elephants arrive and spending a secretive night here would find the experience both awesome and memorable.

Some five hundred miles west of Kitum Cave in the rain-soaked Ruwenzori Mountains, often referred to as the Mountains of the Moon, is another area of note, a place once known for its mountain gorillas, including giant silverbacks whose chest beating can be heard from a long way off. A hundred years ago trophy hunters and museum collectors had no trouble finding the huge primates. Then it was not a question of whether one would see the beasts but rather of deciding which specimens to take and how many. Carl Akeley, noted museum taxidermist and photographer, made five trips into these mountains to collect animals for museum habitat groups. The magnificent African Hall of the American Museum of Natural History in New York was planned, supplied, and developed by Akeley. Even today it still ranks as the world's finest.

Akeley also is credited with inventing the Akeley camera, with which he made the first motion pictures ever taken of mountain gorillas in their natural surroundings. Tragically, Akeley was mauled by a leopard and later died of infection in the Belgian Congo (now Democratic Republic of Congo). He lies buried in the saddle of the Ruwenzoris, the mountains that he knew so well and loved so much. But gorillas occupy these mountains no more.

In Akeley's day big game was everywhere and trophy hunters could pick and choose their quarry at will: lions, leopards, bull elephants with massive tusks, Cape buffalo with great bosses and huge horns. Rhino were also common. When Henry M. Stanley circumnavigated Lake Victoria and explored the Lake Albert–Ruwenzori region (1886–88), he was overwhelmed by the wildness of the area. In his autobiography he said that one of the first sweet and novel pleasures a person can experience in the wilds of Africa is the almost perfect independence; the next is the almost perfect indifference to all things earthly outside camp, one of the most exquisite soul-lulling pleasures a mortal can enjoy. Stanley was speaking of Buganda, the forerunner of modern Uganda, a country that became the envy of Africa.

It seems inconceivable today that this beautiful land so adorned with snow-clad mountains, icy peaks, magnificent forests, and deepwater lakes—all nestled in the western Rift and teeming with game—should have been unknown to the western world until 1856. Unknown, that is, except to one young Greek mathematician-geographer of long ago, a genius of a man stationed in Alexandria and going by the name of Ptolemy. No one except this visionary had any inkling about where the Nile River actually commenced.

Ptolemy was not positive either, but he reasoned that the White Nile had to begin from a series of lakes in Central Africa—lakes fed by a range of snowy peaks he called the Mountains of the Moon. To explain what he meant, he drew a map, a rough sketch, outlining the Nile, the lake country, and the mountains; the document was neither disproved nor accepted, yet it served as a curiosity for seventeen hundred years. From the time of Ptolemy (A.D. 127–51) until 1856 the enig-

Baobab tree near
Victoria Falls.

Gannet rookery on
Bird Island.

Zebra and chimpan-
zees at Jane Goodall's
camp near Lake
Tanganyika.

Maun women in
colorful costumes.

Hyenas feeding on
a dead elephant in
Etosha.

Waterberg Park for Endangered Species was set aside for endangered wildlife species.

Cape fur seal rookery.

The welwitchia; the species hails from the very far past.

Giraffe and zebra in South Africa.

View of canyon from
atop Lesotho.

Rock hyrax atop
Table Mountain.

Jackass penguins at
"the rocks."

View of Cape of
Good Hope.

mas of the Nile and the whole region of Central Africa remained well-kept secrets. Then, finally, in the 1850s the truth began to emerge, thanks first to explorers like Richard Burton, John Speke, and Grant and later to David Livingstone, Samuel Baker, and Henry Stanley. Indeed the Nile was finally shown to originate from Lake Victoria, including the streams flowing out of the snowy, glaciated peaks of Ptolemy's Mountains of the Moon. While today the Pearl of Africa has lost much of its luster, sufficient beauty and bounty remain to warrant a visit.

RUWENZORI NATIONAL PARK, formerly called Queen Elizabeth National Park, is still fine big game country. Herds of zebra, impala, and Uganda kob (antelope) roam its grasslands; giraffe are still seen in large numbers; and Cape buffalo wander about in sizable herds. Lions, cheetahs, and hyenas are common. The most fascinating area of all is the Kazinga Channel, a watercourse connecting Lake Albert with Lake George. Here elephants, hippos, crocodiles, and waterbirds congregate, providing for superb wildlife viewing and photography. A short stay at Mweya Lodge, with its three small but luxurious swimming pools, beautiful grounds, and excellent accommodations and food, comes as a surprise to many tourists. At night zebra and buffalo wander about the grounds and lions make themselves heard.

A day trip in a van along the Kazinga takes one past several lookouts where as many as a thousand hippos can be seen resting and cavorting. The big reddish brown animals yawn, snort, submerge and surface, and jostle for space, their tails slapping the water propeller-fashion as they flush away dung. Although they are usually not especially active by day, there is enough movement and in-

teraction to keep hippo watchers around for hours at a time: huge eyes and nostrils showing, tufted ears twitching, enormous backs wet and heaving, and tick birds picking vermin from wet hides. Massed together, side by side with almost no water showing, hippos remind one of a log jam. Only occasionally do quarrels erupt, even among seven hundred or more jammed behemoths, which speaks well for their diurnal intimacy.

Hippos are among the largest of African mammals, exceeded in size only by the elephant and white rhino. Known technically as *Hippopotamus amphibius,* connoting water-loving, the species is only semi-aquatic. The short-legged, ponderous beasts spend their daytime hours sleeping and cavorting in water but in the early evening they come ashore to feed in marshes, swamps, and grassy uplands, and occasionally to mate. Females have a long gestation period and bear only one calf at a time. Entirely herbaceous, they subsist on grasses and aquatic plants.

Hippos normally weigh from 2,500 to 3,000 pounds, although they can go as high as 5,800 pounds. To keep such a large body functioning, some 120 to 145 pounds of vegetation must be consumed every day. Hippos urinate and defecate a great deal while in the water, so those tails work hard to scatter the waste. The fertilized waters in turn produce rich nitrogen and this in turn stimulates abundant plankton growth and fish production.

Watching hippos lazing in the pools or on banks, one can get the false impression that they are docile. Yet they can be dangerous. Over short distances on land they can bound along at up to twenty-eight miles an hour. Many Africans are killed by hippos when their boats capsize. The large animals are also dangerous to people on foot and lives are lost when people on footpaths near water encounter hippos at night. A hippo has incisors large enough to chomp a person in two. In some places, hippos kill more people each year than do other large mammals, for example, lions or buffalo.

When at last one has had enough of hippo watching, it is time to set off for MURCHISON FALLS NATIONAL PARK. En route to the falls one sees great herds of kob, many foraging in the savannah all the way down to the river's gorge. Here the river gathers frightful speed, narrows, and hurtles down into a chasm just twenty feet wide; its roar is deafening.

Murchison Falls is an impressive cataract. To fully appreciate it, one should see it first from above where the racing waters converge dangerously before plunging wildly into the chasm. Later, one can see the falls from the river below. Around the upper falls one may be lucky to see an angler or two with some very large fish. They are Nile perch, some of the finest eating in Africa, and often run from a hundred fifty to three hundred pounds each.

To cross the Nile one must drive around the falls and cross the river on a small ferry guided by a cable strung from shore to shore. It can take up to ten vehicles per load. Arrangements can also be made to see the lower falls by boarding a special launch. The trip takes about an hour, goes to the foot of the falls, turns around and goes back, giving the observer a different perspective of the plunging and roaring Nile. The launch has been known to collide accidentally with swimming hippos, in encounters forceful enough to shake up the fifty or so passengers aboard and to make the hippos bellow, but serious injuries to the animals seldom occur.

Even the upper Nile is an incredible river at Murchison, where it runs thirty to fourty feet deep and two hundred yards wide. It is the longest river in the world, running for 4,154 miles through jungle, savannah, the treacherous Sud swamps in the Sudan, up through the historic canyons of Egypt, and on to the Mediterranean at Alexandria.

For many centuries the river defied explorers who sought to find its source, people such as Samuel Baker and his young wife, who traveled upriver from Egypt past Khartoum through almost impenetrable swamps all the way to Lake Albert—a journey rivaling Stanley's expedition down the Congo. The Bakers eventually came to the mighty falls. Here, deeply impressed by the roaring cataract, they named the place Murchison Falls in honor of the president of the Royal Geographic Society in Britain. The modern traveler viewing the falls for the first time cannot help but be deeply moved by the scene and the sweep of history it evokes.

Most people coming to Murchison today stay at Para Lodge, not far from the river and within sight of it, a facility noted for its visiting elephants and beautiful sunsets. *Para* means crocodile in the local language and there are still plenty of crocs in the river below the lodge. Elephants often turn on the water spigots on the grounds for an evening bath, then hurry on to the riverbank where, with thousands of Egyptian geese, white pelicans, and yellow-billed storks, they close out an African evening as picturesque and beautiful as can be found.

The journey from Murchison to Kampala is across miles and miles of terrain punctuated by brick-red termite mounds, the structures profiled in Alan and Joan Root's film *Castles of Clay.* Ter-

fig. 18. Murchison Falls on the upper Nile in Uganda.

fig. 19. Nile perch may grow to three hundred pounds and are excellent eating.

fig. 20. *The banks of the Nile near Murchison Falls swarm with waterfowl.*

mite mounds and their inhabitants are special features of local ecology in several other parts of Africa too. To stop at one of them and inspect it thoroughly is a fascinating experience. At the castle we chose to inspect were tracks of many small mammals and a large lizard. Several large holes had been ripped out of the base of the mound and tunnels had been excavated into the interior. Some old holes had been sealed over by the termites. Being daylight, which the termites abhor, we saw only a few individuals scurrying about.

One's approach to a mound should be cautious, knowing that the mounds can be the hiding places of other animals, such as one species of mongoose, monitor lizards, and snakes, including spitting cobras. Active mounds are almost as hard as cement. Indeed they are made of a kind of cemented clay, all pasted together, clay grain by clay grain, with glue from the saliva of worker termites' mouths. No insects may be visible, yet thousands inhabit these colonies. The base of a mound can be so dry and hard that one could ignite a match on it. No wonder elephants use the mounds as scratching posts.

A termite mound is an architectural masterpiece—a remarkable living castle honeycombed with passageways, a nuptial chamber, and several chimneys or flues at the top to provide ventilation as well as natural air conditioning. The queen and king termites and their soldier guardians, together with hordes of workers, inhabit and work in various chambers. Today enough is known about termites to piece together an unbelievable life history.

Termites are not ants, although at one life stage some members develop wings and are erroneously called flying ants or white ants. They belong to the order Isoptera, an old group of quite primitive insects dating back some seventy million years ago. Although there are 188 species of termites, only a small number have developed the ability of boring into wood, the termite trait that can endanger our own structures. These insects first developed in the tropics, where it is warm and usually moist, but have since expanded into temperate zones all over the world.

Some Isoptera have a complex social organization rivaling that of higher-order insects, such as ants and bees. The social organization in a termite castle consists of three classes called castes, each adapted to performing highly specialized tasks. Smallest in number is the reproductive caste, which is made up of an active queen, a king, and a number of additional individuals of both sexes. Should the queen or king die, one of these secondary insects takes its place. Members of this elite group are charged with one function only—reproduction. All necessities of life are provided for them.

The second caste consists of adult soldier termites, all sterile. Their sole job in life is to defend the castle and its termite inhabitants, particularly the queen, whose abdomen may become so egg-laden as to take on the appearance of a fat sausage. Soldiers are armed with powerful mandibles and, for their three-quarter-inch size, are remarkably strong. The soldier group are quite numer-

ous but are vastly outnumbered by the workers, which swarm by the hundreds of thousands in a single mound.

The large caste of workers consists of some sterile adults and many young-stage termites, referred to as nymphs. All of the nymphs in the worker group are sightless, and vision among the adults, as in the soldier caste also, is poor, often degenerating altogether. New termite colonies—which are springing up all the time—are established by a winged group from all three castes. Their wings, however, are lost just as soon as a new termite mound is built. The mounds continue to grow until abandoned.

If one could examine a mound in cross section near the ground, one would see growing in some of the dark inner chambers extensive fungal gardens maintained by the workers. The fungi contain enzymes that help break down the wood cellulose on which the termites feed. Termite digestive apparatus is such that cellulose alone cannot be completely broken down by the insect's digestive tract and so it must be aided by the mushroom mix. Workers scout long distances for plant cellulose. When they find it they gorge themselves and return to the colony, where they regurgitate some cellulose and mix it with the fungal growth. The queen and king are fed from the fungal gardens by workers; soldier termites help themselves at the fungal cafeteria.

Being numerous and succulent in the nymph stage, the insects are preyed upon by ants and larger predators, including reptiles, many kinds of birds from ground hornbills to woodpeckers, and certain nocturnal-feasting mammals. The termite-loving nocturnal aardvark and the aardwolf make nightly visits to the mounds in their territory for termites. The aardvark is especially

fig. 21. A cheetah using a termite mound as a lookout point. Courtesy South African Tourism Board

efficient at tearing into the mounds with its powerful claws. Yet the animal is a judicious feeder, digging out only enough termites to satisfy its immediate hunger. Studies show that aardvarks visit numerous mounds on their nightly circuits but never seriously damage a castle.

The great monitor lizard often makes its abode in one of the chimney flues of a termite mound. The monitor is a daylight feeder, emerging from its castle chimney around daybreak. It has a long forked tongue, like that of a snake, with which it tests the air and the ground for scents. To suddenly see only the fast flicker of this tongue com-

ing out of the top of the mound is like seeing the flashing fork of some prehistoric dragon emerging from a dungeon. Soon this bizarre sight is followed by the slow unveiling of the monitor's head, also somewhat reminiscent of a dragon for those of us accustomed to lizards' being more modest in size.

Thus termites should not be viewed solely as destructive. They perform beneficial tasks, such as improving the soil by recycling the nutrients in dead wood. They create homes for other species and provide nourishment for a wide range of other wildlife and even for people: roasted termites are said to taste somewhat like roasted almonds, but I cannot claim to have tested this.

The beautiful country of Uganda, formerly known as Buganda, has seen many political changes and these have affected its wildlife resources appreciably. Travelers may profit from a brief review of its recent unstable past. In 1894 Britain declared Buganda a protectorate and began to incorporate other areas into what is now Uganda. The move brought together under one administrative roof many different tribes, some of them arch enemies. The Nilotic northern tribes, for example, were different in custom, religion, and language from the southern Bantu peoples.

In 1962 Britain decided to make another change. Buganda and three other kingdoms were to become constitutional monarchies, all within the federated republic of Uganda. Milton Obote of the northern tribe of Lango was chosen temporary president. A year later, however, the king of Buganda, King Freddie, was made the official president.

In 1966 Obote accused Freddie of an attempted overthrow of the central government. Soon federal troops under the command of a young colonel, Idi Amin, moved in and stormed the palace of King Freddie, forcing him into exile. A new constitution was adopted giving great power to the new president, Milton Obote.

But in 1971 Obote himself was ousted and by none other than his own colonel, Idi Amin. What followed was the worst reign of terror ever to befall a modern Third World African nation. Amin was a Muslim and the Buganda people were largely Christian, so immediate friction arose. Amin's reign of madness produced upheaval on many fronts. In April, 1979, Amin was ousted by Tanzanian forces, and while the great human carnage then ended, the liberators brought their own new kind of destruction. While the temporary Ugandan government slowly began to restore some semblance of order in the country, the troops from Tanzania began to pick apart the Pearl of Africa. Elephants were shot by the thousands, not only for ivory but also for meat. Hippos were slaughtered in even greater numbers. Rhino, buffalo, giraffe, antelope, and lion were machine-gunned down everywhere. Part of the problem arose from the fact that the soldiers had not been paid for a long time; part from the marketing of meat and hides. The result was that the mercenaries from the east, although they did rid the country of Amin, also took an incredible toll of wild mammals, birds, and crocodiles in the process.

Out of an estimated population of two thousand elephants in 1970, the total population of these pachyderms by 1977 stood at only a hundred fifty. But more recent reports from biologists in Uganda offer hope. In a country conjured with a high biotic potential (the ability of animals to recover) and with good management, surely some of the big game can be induced to rebound. Today the wildlife is returning, and so are the tourists.

One cannot leave Ptolemy's Mountains of the Moon, however, without at least a brief reference to the volcanic mountains in western Uganda, eastern Zaire, and western Rwanda, where the mountain gorilla clings tenuously to survival. Well before Dr. Dian Fossey began making headlines with her pioneering work with the great apes here, I knew of these mountains and often could see the Virungas, including Mount Visoke (meaning "high mountain" in Slavic), when the mist cleared from the Ruwenzoris in Uganda. Surely, I thought, I could make a trek into the Virungas someday to see and photograph the gorillas. It never came to pass, although I did eventually visit Rwanda.

By then Fossey was becoming well-known, having published an account of her work with mountain gorillas in *National Geographic* magazine. Her article stirred in many people, including a movie producer friend and me, an interest in going. We made contact with Dian at Cornell University but she was reluctant to have too many intrusions into the world of the gorillas; moreover, the local government there soon placed further roadblocks to curtail tour groups, and treks there became impractical.

Dr. Fossey persisted with her research there in Rwanda and after more than eighteen years of studying the gorillas and living among them, achieved substantial acclaim. Dian showed that the big gorillas, even the huge silverback males, were no threat to people—that they were shy, gentle, retiring beasts and needed to be befriended. She worked tirelessly with the apes and got to know each animal in her study group on a first-name basis.

She lived in the high rain forest in a crude two-room corrugated steel cabin and zealously guarded her charges from poachers. She established a gorilla cemetery and buried in it some of the animals that were poached. She indicated to her coworkers that, when she died, she wanted to be buried in a simple grave in this same cemetery and that her plain headstone should read merely, *Nyiramachabelli,* which in the language of the local people means "the woman who lived alone in the forest."

The rest is tragic history. Hacked to death in her camp, presumably by poachers, in late December, 1985, she was quietly laid to rest in her cemetery on New Year's Eve, with some fifty friends and coworkers in attendance. On her fresh grave was placed a temporary stick upon which hung a color picture of her and her gorillas from *National Geographic.*

Dian Fossey left behind a legacy of 240 gorillas, on 12,175-foot Mount Visoke—primates she defended staunchly to the very end. Her devotion to gorillas has been memorialized in the film *Gorillas in the Mist* and will long be remembered.

In recent years the Rwanda government has again permitted small groups to go to the gorilla refuge. The trek to these misty mountains is arduous and there are no guarantees that those making the effort will see the huge shy primates. Conservation efforts, meanwhile, continue, thanks to funding and other help received from around the world.

CHAPTER 9

Desert and Delta

THE KALAHARI AND OKAVANGO

The sprawling Kalahari Desert of southern Africa is a strangely paradoxical world, its wide expanses of thin country, sparse grass, and scrubby bushes suddenly yielding in north-central Botswana to the unique wetland that is the inland delta of the Okavango. Its myriad channels with lush vegetation and much game seem a miracle in the surrounding desert. Little rain falls in the Kalahari; some areas in its southern portion receive almost no rain at all. For endless stretches the land seems to cry out for water. Grasses and scant bushes have a dry, withered look most of the year. But even in this harsh and di>cult environment, the animal and bird life is surprisingly rich. When the infrequent rains do come, they are often tumultuous—dramatic thunderstorms are characteristic. Water churns down usually dry watercourses and large flatland depressions or pans fill with water. Patches of terrain quickly green up, transforming the desert briefly into verdant pasture.

The Kalahari is the third largest desert in Africa. In point of antiquity, however, it is said to be the oldest desert in the world, some parts dating back two hundred fifty to four hundred million years. To appreciate this desert, one must set foot in it. Then the harshness softens, the fear slowly lessens, and the beauty of a difficult land begins to show. Deserts are not for everyone. The sensitive desert transplant Joseph Wood Krutch (once a New Yorker) said of Arizona that the desert has no middle ground—one either hates it or learns to love it.

The Kalahari has several distinct faces. The southeastern third is a mixture of semiarid grassland, or savannah, interspersed with leached-out salt pans (slight depressions that are devoid of visible plants but periodically get filled with water). The southwestern portion is the driest, its vegetation the sparsest, a landscape of slightly rolling sand dunes and dry riverbeds. These areas make up another third and constitute the so-called *extreme* desert. Here almost no rain falls. The northern Kalahari is semiarid but contains the astonishing swamp called the Okavango Delta, an immense wetland that sustains a wealth of wildlife. The contrast between the profusion of the Okavango and the struggle for life in the desert beyond it makes the delta seem all the more a miracle.

The Okavango Delta is not easy to reach. It is remote and isolated. It has resisted development; thus the area remains gloriously wild and untouched. Little wonder, then, that it is such a powerful attraction for those who love wild places. Dr. Bruce Hargraves, one-time teacher at Chancellor College, Malawi, once remarked that, of all the places in the world he'd most love to visit, the Kalahari and its fabulous Okavango Delta rate at the top. He noted that this desert is the least disturbed, semiarid desert environment in the world—rich, ecologically fascinating, and unmatched in plant and animal life, a biologist's heaven on earth.

To see this desert properly, or any desert for that matter, one first needs to have the right attitude toward it. A desert is extremely sensitive to human intrusion. Today, cattle ranching in the Kalahari poses a threat, and there has been a huge and roaring controversy in conservation circles for years, with fences built to restrict wildlife movement (in order to prevent spread of disease to cattle) interfering with game movements and resulting in mass deaths. Indeed, Botswana has been working on a major national conservation plan.

The Kalahari extends over much of southern and southwestern Africa, including parts of Namibia and covering roughly 85 percent of the sparsely populated country of Botswana. Most of this desert is flat, monotonous, with vast stretches of thinly clad grassland mixed with barren openings, or pans, some of which may be fringed with low acacia bushes. There are no purple-colored plateaus or highlands similar to what one sees in Kenya or Arizona. Even though the desert is harsh and rainfall is extremely limited, generally occurring for a month or so in November–December and again for ten days to two months in March–April, a surprising variety of game is to be found. The animals are especially numerous near the fringes of the Okavango, although it is not uncommon to see mammals and birds far from water.

Springbok often wander in the driest areas. The seventy- to eighty-pound springbok is similar to the Thomson's gazelle of Kenya and Tanzania but is quite larger. During the time of Livingstone, or even as recently as the days of Martin and Osa Johnson (1920s–30s), springbok migrated across the Kalahari by the thousands (today their numbers and movements are more limited). Often they appeared in such densely packed masses that other animals crossing their path were trampled to death or forced to go along with them. The movements apparently coincided with the rhythm of drought and rainfall, taking the animals to pans holding water and rangelands bearing enough to eat. Periodically, if not annually, these migrations often ended in disaster as disease (generally anthrax), starvation, flood waters, and predators took their toll. At other times thousands died when severe drought forced many herds to travel to the sea to drink deadly saltwater.

Crossing this desert by dirt road, one may see a great flock of ostriches on the move. The birds, often all young or nearly full grown, travel in single file across the open pans and are quite a sight. As evening settles over the Sowa and Makgadikgadi pans, the big red sun sinks low over the desert and creates a rich mosaic of color in place of the daylight glare.

The nights are cold and remarkably clear, with fiery meteorites streaking across the sky. Here the Southern Cross is usually plainly visible. Often one's ears pick up the unmistakable *Aaaah . . . UGH! Aaaah . . . UGH!* of a lone brown hyena hunting somewhere in the darkness (this long-haired form is the more common hyena in the Kalahari). This hyena is fairly silent, compared to the spotted hyena, having no whoop call. The hunting call, more staccato-like, is a little different from the voice of the spotted species one hears in Tanzania and Kenya.

All morning and well into noon the road winds northwestward across the Kalahari pans. During the infrequent short wet periods, the pans run pink with flamingos. Much game gathers around the water holes and this gives the desert a remarkably lively look. Springbok then pack the pans solid. In lesser numbers wander the gemsbok. This is a large antelope reaching four hundred fifty pounds, closely resembling the beisa oryx in Samburu in Kenya, but here in the Kalahari it is found only in widely separate habitats. A dry land species of the Kalahari and parts of Namibia, it is able to go without drinking for long periods, securing its moisture requirements from the plants it eats, including forbs and grasses, which take up moisture in the cool nights when relative humidity increases. Eaten early in the morning they offer quite a lot of moisture. The gemsbok is highly adapted to the high temperatures of the desert.

To protect the gemsbok and other desert wildlife, the government of Botswana has wisely set aside the Kalahari Gemsbok National Park, which meets up with an already existing similar park in South Africa (see the chapter on South Africa for more information about this park in Botswana and South Africa). Northeast of the

Central Kalahari Game Reserve the desert stretches endlessly, like a grassy sea, flowing toward the enormous Makgadikgadi salt pans, a vast white ink-splash on the desert. When the October or November rains come, these pans fill up with rainwater and become shallow lakes, attracting hordes of ducks, geese, and other waterbirds. Thousands of wildebeest and zebra also congregate here, along with springbok and gemsbok. Seen in daylight they flow like a mottled living carpet across the heat-shimmering Kalahari landscape. For a time the herds move in a wide sweeping arc around the pans, drinking often and nibbling on what scant grasses they can find. Then as the waters recede, they travel northwestward toward Lake Ngami, making a slow migratory journey toward the sweet waters of the benevolent Okavango Delta.

David Livingstone reached Lake Ngami in 1849, when he began making extensive trips into the Kalahari from the mission station at Kuruman (now in South Africa), some four hundred miles away and not far from the present-day town of Upington on the Orange River. One can visit the Moffat mission at Kuruman—there is a little museum there. The young preacher–adventurer traveled in a wagon drawn by oxen, moving across the desert from one water hole to another, studying animals, birds, and plants. Generally the water holes were revealed to him by friendly nomadic Bushmen who hunted in the area. It was during these delightful and sometimes extended excursions, including a few with his wife and children, that Livingstone became a self-taught naturalist and an expert bird observer.

The game and bird life, as well as the reptiles and insects of the Makgadikgadi, proved to be so rich that the present Botswana government deemed it wise to set aside here a huge game reserve of some six thousand square miles—larger than the Serengeti and Mara combined. In the wide-open, gently rolling plains north of here, dotted with islands of palm trees, it was not uncommon to count upward of five to ten thousand zebra and wildebeest in a single day. And out of the tawny wild recesses came the springbok, gemsbok, and hartebeest to stand or flow against the background of a salt-colored horizon—a spectacle clearly similar to what one still sees in the Tanzania-Kenya plains and the southern savannah of the Sudan.

Today, as in the days of Livingstone, one can still come upon small groups of native people, the Bushmen or San, stalking game. They know the water holes well and wait, concealed, for unsuspecting animals to appear. How these people have traditionally survived in this desert wilderness has been the object of much study and more than one film. The small-statured Bushmen of the central Kalahari Desert are not related to any other tribe in Botswana. The average Bushman stands about five feet or less in height and weighs barely ninety pounds.

The Bushmen historically were nomadic, moving from place to place constantly, subsisting by hunting and plant gathering. Water was so difficult to find most of the time that for weeks these people relied on the juices of plants and animals. Their traditional diet included primarily plant matter but also birds, snakes, insects, ostrich eggs, and the occasional freshly killed big game animal. Their knowledge of plants was, and is, astounding.

The Kalahari Bushmen erected no villages because they were on the move all the time. But they did sometimes construct simple structures when they remained in one place for a while. They had no leaders, no chiefs, but simply roamed in small

bands from eight to twelve members, sometimes in groups numbering up to forty or fifty. Personal property was restricted to tools and weapons, skin blankets, and decorative items—lovely ostrich eggshell beadwork, for example. There were several Bushmen tribes, each tribe having its own language; Bushman languages—distinguished by a whole series of different kinds of clicks—have now received attention from linguists.

The weary road traveler rolling across the Kalahari finally reaches the town of Maun. Here the desert suddenly becomes an oasis of green vegetation, lots of water, and numbers of people. Several rivers flow near the hamlet, all carrying water so clear, so sky-blue that you want to rush out and drink it. Women show their origins through colorful great headdresses and hoop skirts. And safari vehicles and trucks scurry about this frontier outpost, which buzzes with activity as the principal jump-off point for the fabulous Okavango Delta.

The delta, a seven-thousand-square-mile triangle of shallow freshwater, a strange moving river of grass, rich in plant and animal life, relieves the dryness of the Kalahari. The source of the water is the Okavango River, deriving from the mountains of eastern Angola. The river flows southeastward for more than five hundred miles, finally spilling out across the desert in a vast fan-shaped freshwater delta, then is swallowed up by the desert. The delta forms a sort of rough triangle measuring about a hundred miles on each side. As the river spills out over the desert, it creates thousands of channels, luxuriant papyrus-lined islets punctuating the many fingers of wetland. Some of the islands are large enough to support big game. The lesser islands are habitat for smaller game, such as warthog, reedbuck, lechwe (an antelope), and the rare aquatic antelope called the sitatunga. And all areas have their share of water-birds: plovers, rails, ducks, geese, coots, egrets, jacanas, herons, flamingos, and fish eagles. Many small reed birds are present and some are star-tlingly handsome, like the flashing blue-green-backed malachite kingfisher and the carmine bee-eater.

From Maun one can fly into the Okavango in-terior, where several camps cater to visitors. As we flew low over the vast world of islands and chan-nels, we saw wildebeest, elephant, and lechwe on the larger islands. Large flocks of cattle egrets sailed over the open water like white clouds, dazzling in the sunlight for a moment, then swept away across the endless maze of waterways. Xaxaba Camp, our destination, on the western edge of an unnamed island, was scarcely visible as we approached. We landed on a tiny grass airstrip and were taken to a reed-lined camp shaded by a large tree near the water's edge. The giant strangler fig, true to its name, was well on its way to strangling a smaller adjacent tree.

Early in the evening, before sunset, we boarded an aluminum boat in a small group. With our guide, the camp director, in the bow, standing, and a Tswana boatman at the outboard controls, we took off up a broad channel for a firsthand close-up view of the Okavango. Moving swiftly up one channel and down another, with the guide giving hand directions to his motorman, the group was given "one heck of a ride." After a fifteen-minute breezy run, we halted at a small lagoon as evening shadows lengthened.

"Fish eagles," announced the guide in his Brit-ish accent. "Be real quiet." A pair of the birds were high in a tree, much too difficult for pictures but clearly visible through binoculars. One of the

eagles issued forth from the tree, made a wide arc in the air, swooped down, grabbed up a fish with its talons, and was away flapping noisily against the water to rise again. It was a beautiful aerial performance and we were promised we could re-turn in the morning when the light would be better for pictures.

At dinner in a simple, open-sided reed shelter, the manager announced that there would be an-other boat trip into the marshes that night and warned all planning to go to wear heavy jackets. Okavango nights in July and August can be quite cold, dropping down into the upper forties.

At 9:30 P.M., in the black of night, a boatload of adventurers again set out down a series of dark channels, the guide once more standing in the bow and giving directions, this time with a pow-erful torchlight. After we had been zigging and zagging for nearly thirty minutes, the guide sud-denly began flashing his light back and forth onto one spot in the reeds. The boatman cut the mo-tor and we lunged to a halt, then drifted slowly and quietly toward shore. We all held our breath as the guide's light continued to play on a small clump of reeds. Silently the boat eased to where the beam illuminated the reedy shore, now just feet away.

"Everyone be still," the guide cautioned. "Real still. Don't even breathe." Then we saw: one, two, four, eight—fourteen tiny birds, all sitting mo-tionless on a single horizontal reed stem. Were they for real? Presently several birds blinked; oth-ers moved their heads a little. They stayed just where they were, as if mesmerized by the light. It never fazed the birds one bit. How the guide was able to spot them in their reedy wilderness was a mystery to us.

The central Okavango offers the visitor an opportunity to experience the wildness of a trip without motors or groups. One can be poled by a Tswana guide in a *mokoro,* or dugout, gliding down miles of shallow channels between green walls of reeds to camp out for a night or two. Sleeping on the ground under the stars with wild game moving about in the darkness can be deeply moving, especially with lions and spotted hyenas sounding their presence and possibly investigating more closely. Or one can elect to go by motorboat deep into a watery universe, some seventy miles away, and spend the night on an isolated islet, listening to grunting hippos feeding on lush vegetation, some barely thirty yards away, perhaps wondering if one's sleeping bag is in the way of

their evening peregrinations. The ultimate is to be suddenly awakened by the shriek of a baboon in a nearby tree as a leopard collects a meal.

These are brief moments that capture the very quintessence of wildness—moments in a wetland eden such as exists nowhere else in Africa. The Okavango offers a distinctive safari experience, with its mix of aerial wildlife viewing en route into the delta, spotting from boats, some walking, and accommodation in relatively rustic camps. Knowing that beyond the life-giving waters stretches the wide Kalahari Desert and that far, far away lie major cities gives one a sense of Africa primeval that is hard to match anywhere else.

CHAPTER 10

Namibia

A SYMPHONY IN SAND AND ROCK

Of all the wild lands of Africa, none can compare in stark natural beauty and isolated wildness to those found in Namibia. Here in the driest of deserts sprawl remote rocky mountains, canyons, and escarpments; record-high sand dunes and immense gravel plains; a cold coastal Atlantic wilderness that is truly a different world; and acacia bushlands and great salt pans, in places where rainfall increases slightly. Namibia is a country of sparse human population and fantastic scenic wonders that must be seen to be believed.

Wedged between Angola to the north, the more vegetated Kalahari Desert to the east, South Africa to the south, and the cold surf-blasted Atlantic coast on the west, Namibia gained its independence under a United Nations mandate in 1990. Dedicated to democracy, the rule of law, and the free enterprise system, Namibia is a land of rebirth and resurrection, both politically and environmentally. Namibia's German flavor comes from its German colonial past, which makes the place very distinctive and makes it feel entirely

different from other African countries. Close to the center of the country is its capital, Windhoek; this is the point of entry for most visitors, served by air from Europe. To the north lie the Waterberg Park for Endangered Species and Etosha National Park. To the south and west is the Namib Desert proper, including the Namib-Naukluft National Park; the rugged desert landscape is cut through by the Fish River Canyon, dry riverbeds, and scant vegetation—plant life is dominated here by the strange-looking kokerboom or quiver tree, uncommon elsewhere. In all four regions groups of wild animals, such as springbok, gemsbok, and zebra, can be seen.

The road out of the city is black-topped and quickly takes one into open countryside with large, fenced cattle ranches stretching away on both sides. The landscape is undulating semiarid savannah studded with acacia trees and with occasional windmills pumping water into troughs for livestock. Here and there springbok and ostriches are seen.

WATERBERG PARK FOR ENDANGERED SPECIES, some two hundred fifty miles north, lies in the direction of Etosha National Park. This is an isolated wilderness mesa, an oval plateau surrounded by palisade-like cliffs. The area embraces some one hundred thousand acres of highland savannah and scrub. The steep sandstone cliffs around the plateau make the area virtually poacher-proof. The only access road, on the east side, is tightly controlled by park officials. What makes Waterberg significant is that the whole table-top wilderness is a sanctuary set aside for endangered wildlife; both species of rhino are here, as are roan, sable, and tsessebe (three species of antelope). Also found in the refuge are kudu, impala, gemsbok, giraffe, brown hyena, cheetah, leopard, warthog, and baboon. Namibia

has Africa's greatest remaining cheetah population. The Cape buffalo has been reintroduced. Snakes include the python, dwarf python, and three notoriously poisonous species, the black mamba, boomslang, and puff adder.

More than two hundred species of birds have been recorded at Waterberg. Black eagles and other birds of prey have been seen, as well as rosy-faced lovebirds, crimson-breasted shrikes, hornbills, and doves.

Significantly, too, Waterberg is home to the only breeding colony of Cape vultures in Namibia. Because of a special vulture feeding station in the preserve, some twenty birds are now being maintained (down from a one-time population of five hundred). Before the preserve was created in 1972, various out-of-control activities

fig. 22. A sparsely vegetated riverbed courses before the impressive sand dunes of western Namibia, part of the Namib-Naukluft National Park, the largest in Africa.

and natural occurrences decimated the vulture population.

The highland plateau and the southern foothills are graced with diversified vegetation. The upper zone harbors many deciduous trees and deep-rooted acacias. There are large stretches of savannah and scrub, ideal for browsers and grazers. The foothills around the government-operated rest camp (in all the Namibian and South African national parks, the camps are operated by park personnel rather than by private concessionaires, in contrast to some of the parks in East Africa) and the flats below support sycamore figs and evergreen trees, including umbrella and swarthaak (blackthorn) acacias. Along trails near the camp and around several springs are mongooses and noisy francolins. Pied crows begin calling at dawn and various doves sound their melancholy notes all day long. The atmosphere here is one of undisturbed wildness. Little wonder there is such great hope for Waterberg. A museum and nature education center are in the works here at the De la Bat camp.

Waterberg has an interesting history. It once featured prominently in the wars between the German colonists and the Herero tribe. Bushmen lived in the area until 1967 and some of their engravings are present. Demara people lived at the site of the new camp during the last century, and Herero cattle herders moved into the area around 1850. The first whites to visit Waterberg were the explorers Anderson and Galton in 1851. A police post was set up by the German colonial authorities after 1896, and in 1904 German Schutztruppe defeated the Hereros in a decisive battle. Graves of Schutztruppe who died in the fighting can be seen in the cemetery below the camp. In 1908 the German authorities built a police station, now known as the Rasthaus, which served as police offices until 1955.

Geologically the park consists mainly of a plateau of compacted layered sandstone (the Etjo formation) formed about 200–180 million years ago. The plateau is the remnant of a much larger plateau which extended over a wider area. The sandstone at the top of the plateau tends to act like a sponge, so there is little surface water, but several springs emerge here and at the base of the southern cliffs. Some spectacular rock formations can be seen in places along the escarpment, including *pillar, toadstool,* and *honeycomb* formations. Dinosaurs once roamed the area and left their footprints in the red rocks.

On coolish evenings in March when the sun begins to cast a golden glow over the brick-red cliffs, the view from several craggy overlooks atop the sanctuary is solemn and breathtaking. Often a black eagle can be seen soaring in wide circles, peering down on an old but sill beautiful world— a rare place where everything seems harmonious in nature and man is but an alien visitor in a strange eden.

ETOSHA NATIONAL PARK is one of the continent's greatest game parks and another notable sanctuary of hope in southwestern Africa. Etosha lies 125 miles northwest of Waterberg in northern Namibia and is not too far from the Angola border. Covering a vast flatland of nearly six thousand square miles (larger than Tanzania's Serengeti), Etosha was proclaimed a game preserve in 1907 by the German governor, von Linderquist, after it had been a hunter's paradise for many years. The heart of the park is Etosha Pan, discovered in 1815 by Sir Francis Galton and Charles Anderson. According to some geologists the present pan was an inland lake millions of years ago, fed by the Kunene River. In recent times the river changed its course to the sea and the pan shrank to its present size (60 miles in length north to south by 140 miles wide). It goes bone-dry in the rainless months from March to October, then only vast stretches of sun-baked, cracked mud and alkaline soda powder are visible, and this extends for hundreds of square miles all around. In 1952 a beginning was made to develop the area as a game park with three main camps along the southern fringe. A fourth camp is in the planning stage. Taking the character of old-time German forts, the three modern facilities—Namutoni in the east, Halali in the central sector, and Okaukuejo in the west—feature bungalows (roundavels), tent areas, swimming pools, and eating facilities. They are first-class government-operated rest camps and are adequately fenced from marauding predators and dangerous other big game. But game observation places in the park are many, and good gravel roads connect the three camps. These are spaced about fifty miles apart. Game viewing is from motor vehicles, but no open roof hatches are permitted. Just outside of Okaukuejo the visitor can look into a water hole where, in the dry season, many lions make their kill.

Most big game animals abound year-round in Etosha, but the large concentration really occur during the dry season when mixed herds gather around the water holes. Elephants, eland, zebra, springbok, impala, giraffe, gemsbok, kudu, and hartebeest are then common sights, as are lion, cheetah, hyena, mongoose, and jackal. Baboons walk around everywhere, and ostriches are plentiful, oftentimes in large flocks. The black-faced impala, once rare and recently reintroduced, are now frequent sights around Namutoni and Om-

bika. Black rhino require a bit of scouting as do sightings of Damara dik-dik, usually best seen in the afternoon. When the rains come, the game animals scatter widely as water then is readily available everywhere, including the pans. Many of the park's eight thousand elephants go trekking northeast, some even out of the park in response to long established migratory patterns rooted deep in their genes. Springbok also migrate in large herds.

An unfortunate game population-control factor, now closely monitored by biologists, is anthrax. This disease takes a good many elephants and zebra during the dry season. The stagnant waters here and there are full of deadly bacilli, and browsing and grazing herbivores often succumb to it. Carnivores are not affected.

Birdlife in Etosha is rich with 325 species reported. Great concentrations of Abdin's storks can be seen at times feeding on locusts, and flamingos flock to the pans to breed during the wet season. The kori bustard and guinea fowl are often observed, as are unusual flutterings of noisy black korhaan. Social weavers who build enormous nests in the few trees are common sightings on the grassy fringes of the pans. The chanting goshawk and tawny eagle are noted frequently, as are the lilac-breasted rollers, clapper larks, doves, francolin, sand grouse, and the colorful crimson-breasted shrike.

As far as vegetation, Etosha has many diverse plant species. The pan is barren except for grass in localized areas. Around the perimeter are extensive grass plains and salt-loving grasses and shrubs. The deciduous shrubs consist mainly of mopane, but to the east this gives way to mixed woodland of tamboti, "appelblaar," wild figs, wild dates, maroela, makalani palms, various thorn trees, and a variety of other shrubs. West of Okaukuejo is a Haunted Forest, a dense stand of *Moringa ovalifolia.* It is the only place where such a concentration of these unusual looking, ghost-like trees occur on the plain. Normally they prefer rocky slopes or mountains. These trees are also limited to Namibia.

Leaving Etosha is normally a regretful moment but knowing the plans of our new driver-guide, Hank Coetsee, we knew that more exciting places were yet to come. Ahead lie the red rocks volcanic country, the Skeleton Coast, and the fabulous Namib-Naukluft Park.

DEMARA REGION. In this rugged, dry area southwest of Etosha one often sees small herds of mountain zebra. They are in a special reserve and appear extremely shy. The species has stripes larger than those of the Grevy's but narrower than that of Burchell's, a difficult variety to tell apart. They have short cross strips along the backbone on the rump and whitish bellies on the bottomside. Here one often sees individual springbok and gemsbok, usually wandering around on dry hillsides and in arid stream beds.

PETRIFIED FOREST. Halfway between Kamanjab in the northern region and the Skeleton Coast Park is a unique fossil area called the Petrified Forest. It is strongly reminiscent of the Petrified National Monument in Arizona and just as old, dating back some 180–200 million years. Here sections of large tree stems and broken log sections are strewn about, with many log pieces clearly showing their annual rings. Acres and acres of petrified rocks litter the landscape in a bizarre setting very much like the Chinla Formation in Arizona. A modest guardpost and a lone atten-

dant are the only reminders in our approaching twenty-first century of a world once sunk deep into the Tertiary Period long, long ago.

Around the general area of the Petrified Forest, now a national monument, there are dry mountain crags, red rock chimneys, black volcanic craters, many with early Bushmen engravings, which suggest a paradise for the probing geologists and anthropologists. Farther southward across the rocky arid stretches where seemingly nothing grows, one suddenly comes across the rarest desert plant in the world. It is *Welwitschia mirabilis,* a fossil plant with only two frondlike leathery leaves and a strange six-foot stem, a structure which dies back during extreme dry periods. These rare, living fossil plants are said to reach the incredible age of two thousand or more years.

The SKELETON COAST is a barren, hostile, and desolate environment characterized by rolling surf, seaside dunes, and wide gravelly coastal plains. In some places the flatlands extend forty miles inland before the high Namib sand dunes begin. The coastal waters are both rocky and sandy, very cold because of the Antarctic current sweeping upward from the south polar sea. Many shipwrecks can be seen up and down the coast, hence its name, Skeleton Coast. Countless seamen who survived the wrecks went ashore vainly searching for fresh water and food, only to succumb to the merciless desert. No rain falls here, but heavy fogs are frequent and bring some moisture to dune plants and animals found inland.

The southern section of the Skeleton Coast is a coastal recreation area, and surf fishing is both enticing and rewarding. Some fishermen with four-wheel drives towing dune buggies come from as far away as the Transvaal, a thousand miles away, just to surf fish for rock bass, kingfish, and other sporting fishes. But they must bring their own tentage, gear, food, water, and petrol with them. The middle section of the Skeleton Coast is a national park, remote, wild, lonely except for the sea birds that ply the area and some flamingoes who sometimes wade in the coastal waters. The upper north third of the Skeleton Coast is roadless, a true seaside wilderness. It sweeps northward hundreds of miles to the Angola border. Fly-in safaris to the area can be arranged from the quaint city of Swakopmund and from Windhoek.

North of Swakopmund a *salt-mac* road (sand-gravel track packed down from sprayed and evaporated salt water) parallels the coast for several hun-

dred miles. At Cape Cross a sanctuary for Cape fur seals has been established and here at times as many as eighty-eight thousand noisy, smelly seals can be seen. They pack the coastal rocks solid.

Walvis Bay is still an enclave of South Africa in Namibia, a shipping and fish processing port. A desert track detours around it and heads east sixty miles across the bleak desert to an isolated desert research station. Here biologists Dr. H. Berry and a small staff run one of the most remote desert facilities on earth—and the only true desert research station in the world. Despite the bleakness of the Namib-Naukluft area, more plants and animals have learned to survive in this desert environment than anyone might believe.

fig. 23. Dry Naukluft Mountains in western Namibia.

fig. 24. Adventuring in the Namib wilderness, where sand dune mountains are the loftiest, longest, and largest in the world . . . and the most picturesque.

The NAMIB-NAUKLUFT NATIONAL PARK—comprising a total of 12,103,000 acres, the fourth largest national park in the world and largest in Africa—traverses some of the driest, fiercest, yet most beautiful dry wilderness lands in the world. Occasional visitors make stops at Sesreim Canyon, Solitaire, Sossuvie (a place of *rare* standing water) and, finally, choose a remote campsite under a camel-thorn tree (*Acacia eranuva*) in a picturesque sand dune mountain setting some sixty miles away.

One morning we took off for the big dunes, stopping now and then to photograph, first a lone gemsbok at the foot of a large sweeping pink-colored dune and then five gemsbok in a row before another majestic dune. They were far away and in the intense midmorning sunlight looked like tiny white ghosts lined against the backdrop of immense hills of pinkish sand hills.

Our final stop was a camel-thorn old dry riverbed. A range of dune mountains had built up to form a dam across an ancient river which once flowed out to sea. The thorn trees provided the only shade in the area and we picnicked beneath them. The trees have taproots said to go down a hundred feet through the sand to find moisture. It was a perfectly magnificent stop, quiet, fiercely primeval, gloriously wild. We finally took off in our Land Rover for a romp over the great sand mountains, got stuck in the sand on the crest of one dune, and began to shovel ourselves out. It was so deathly hot at midday on the dunes that two of us decided to promptly hike back down over the sand hills to our picnic spot. Jan and our other companion, Dr. John Hewston, stayed back shoveling away. An hour after reaching the rest stop, we heard a motor vehicle grinding away out of sight. Eventually our two more adventurous souls appeared—a welcome sight. It proved a superlative adventure with superlative wild dunes imprinted solidly in our minds for the rest of our lives. Namibia and the Namib-Naukluft had done its best for us.

The Namib sand dunes are immense in size, often towering a thousand feet into the clear blue desert sky. They extend for more than a thousand miles north to the Angola border, the wildest sand mountains in the world.

Despite the fierceness of the Namib, some life does exist on the summits of these monster dunes. Dune ants and headstander beetles emerge at night and feed on specks of vegetated detritus blown in on the foggy winds. The headstander lifts its abdomen high and eventually collects tiny globs of moisture on the end of its body which finally trickles down to its mouth.

In recent years researchers have discovered and photographed desert elephants and lions traveling over the dunes to quench their thirst in freshwater springs located at the foot of some dunes, water holes fed by subterranean aquifers which originate hundreds of miles away in Angola. The elephants come also to bathe and feed on green plants around the springs, the lions to prey on the Cape fur seals in a coastal rookery nearby. It is, by all sense of measurement, "a wild Eden" rare in Africa.

CHAPTER II

South Africa

ITS WONDROUS WILDS AND REFUGES OF HOPE

South Africans like to promote their nation as "a world in one country." For anyone who has traveled widely in this most southerly of African nations, this is hardly an exaggeration. This subtropical nation, anchor of an incredible subcontinent, has more going for it than anyone can possibly imagine. This applies to landscapes, wild lands, modern cities and towns, transport, industry and economy, the diversity of people and cultures, and a natural resources base that is the envy of all Africa if not the world. If South Africa is anything to the domestic and foreign traveler, it is a world of scenic beauty, wild wonder, surprising modernity, and advanced resource management all wrapped up in one remarkable package.

To begin with, South Africa is no small country. It is larger than Texas and Oklahoma combined and bigger than France, England, and Sweden together, encompassing an area of 471,000 square miles. Distances are great. As the black eagle might fly, diagonally, it is 1,500 miles from the border between the Kruger National Park and Mozam-

bique in the northeast to the Atlantic coast in the northwestern Cape Province. Elevations range from sea level to an altitude of over eleven thousand feet in the mountains of Lesotho (an independent enclave country, not part of South Africa), where in winter months (June and July) the snows can run deep and temperatures plummet to zero. While at most lower elevations frost does not occur, homes require heat. Because South Africa's physiographic features are so diverse, the climate, particularly rainfall, varies considerably. Thus the vegetation is extremely diverse, and so is the fauna.

Historically, settlement in South Africa occurred mostly in the sixteenth, seventeenth, and eighteenth centuries, with colonization credited mostly to the Dutch and English. In the 1800s much of South Africa's interior began to be settled. The Boer War of 1899 to 1902 was a bitter conflict between the Boer (Dutch) farmers and the English. The issue was gold and diamonds, both found in the latter years of the nineteenth century. Once these were found the British wanted the interior and were no longer satisfied to let the Boers hang onto it. The conflict ended with the former two British colonies and two Boer republics becoming a single British dominion.

The official languages spoken in South Africa include English and Afrikaans, the Dutch-derived language of the settlers, and there are many dialects and numerous tribal languages. The country is traditionally considered to have three ethnic groups: black, which includes Zulus; Caucasian or white; and colored, which includes those of Indian, oriental, and Muslim extraction. Blacks are in the great majority in South Africa. The whites come in a distant second.

The four former republics that became the four provinces—Transvaal, Orange Free State, Natal, and Cape Province—are now no longer. South Africa has been redivided into nine provinces; only Natal and Orange Free State are much as they were, except that they are now called Kwa-Zulu-Natal and Free State. Since I traveled while the original four provinces were still intact, I will use those provinces in my discussions.

TRANSVAAL. The most northerly of the four former provinces in South Africa, Transvaal was a large, landlocked area, bounded by Botswana, Zimbabwe, Mozambique, Natal, Swaziland, Lesotho, Orange Free State, and the Cape Province. The province was noted for its great beauty, extensive agricultural lands, immense mineral wealth, and abundant wildlife. Much of the eastern Transvaal was subtropical lowveld, a region of rolling farmlands, savannah, and woodlands, famous in Africa and the world over for the presence of some of the country's foremost game parks.

The northern Transvaal and parts of the west were identified by open plains, high mountains, and native forests. A grassy plateau, generally known as the highveld, comprised most of the central and southwestern Transvaal. On the highveld plateau in the southern part of the province, near Johannesburg, one could see heavy industrialization, the most highly developed area in South Africa. The Vaal River, principal tributary of the Orange River, formed the boundary between Transvaal and the former Orange Free State. The Vaal Dam created an immense reservoir, which continues to provide water for the surrounding industries and the urban complex; it also serves as an important recreation area.

Transvaal, of course, was big game country and here Kruger National Park was the premier game reserve. Kruger is the largest national park in the country and one of the biggest in Africa. More animal and bird species are known to occur here than in any other national park in Africa. All members of the big five are present: elephant, rhino, Cape buffalo, lion, and leopard. At the time I visited, lions numbered about five hundred and the elephant population was given as about eight thousand.

Unfortunately, each year some elephants must be culled to keep the numbers in balance with the food supply. The operation is a distasteful one but wise management decrees it must be done. A helicopter is used to select groups for culling and a shooter in the chopper fires tranquilizing darts into all the animals. Then personnel on the ground dispatch the immobilized animals with a rifle. A few young are captured and sent to other preserves. All parts of the elephant are utilized: the hide used for leather products, the bones pulverized for bone meal, and the flesh sold and

fig. 25. A gang of hippos cavort in a pool in Kruger National Park.

canned. The tusks are safely stored for later possible use.

Kruger has a number of camp facilities, good roads, and vista points, but no roof hatches on vehicles are permitted. Adjoining Kruger are several private game preserves, such as Mala Mala, Sabi Sand, and others, where big game can be viewed from open vehicles. They are sophisticated facilities and cater to every kind of taste on the part of the visitor. Close-up views of elephant, rhino, lion, leopard, zebra, buffalo, giraffe, impala, wildebeest, kudu, and other antelope are common.

Kruger is a classic place for a do-it-yourself safari, where visitors are safe, gasoline and supplies are available, and camping is permitted. Also, fly-in guided minibus tours of a few days are available. Professional photographers repeatedly decree Kruger a favorite destination for photographing a wide range of species on a longish stay that is not too expensive.

ORANGE FREE STATE. This former province, mostly rolling and golden, was a region of elevated flatlands, farms, mountains, and bushveld. Sheep and goat ranching predominated,

fig. 26. Steenbok in Kruger National Park. Courtesy South African Tourism Board

Wild Edens

especially where the land was drier and the soils had a lot of reddish oxide in them. Some mountains, the Drakensberg, formed a fringe to the province and bore snow in winter, giving the name "Little Switzerland" to the area.

The only national park found in this former province is the Golden Gate Highlands National Park, a small area of some twenty-five thousand acres of high grassland noted for its sour grasses and many species of wildflowers, bulbs, and shrubs. From springtime to autumn one can see dazzling displays of fire, arum, and Easter lilies, red hot pokers, watsonias, and daisies. The tree known as oudehout in Afrikaans, which translates to "old wood" because of its gnarled appearance,

and other indigenous trees flourish in the ravines. Mammals include springbok, grey rhebok, oribi, zebra, and eland, in addition to some species endemic to South Africa, including the vaal rhebok, blesbok, and the rare black wildebeest, that cannot be seen outside the country. Over 140 bird species are present, including the black eagle and the bearded vulture or lammergeyer, which resembles an eagle more than a vulture. Hiking trails are extensive and lead to majestic overlooks in the mountains, many across deep, open valleys and up into high points, some of which rise to nine thousand feet above sea level.

There are also a number of private game preserves. Rhino, impala, eland, and black wildebeest can be seen in the Willem Pretorius Game Reserve, operated by the provincial nature conservation authorities.

Traveling through the former Orange Free State one saw green valleys, cultivated fields, rolling hills and escarpments, mountains, and a neat countryside splashed with villages, towns, and small cities. There were some small rivers and lakes and considerable pasturage. If it happened to be springtime or autumn the bird life was particularly prevalent, notably pied crows, larks, sunbirds, bee-eaters, doves, and weaverbirds.

Occasionally, across the wide open golden fields, particularly grain fields, red-billed queleas would suddenly appear in great flocks. They give the impression of swarming locusts or bees. When they gather in cloudlike masses, they are a spectacle to behold. One is baffled at how the tiny birds can fly so swiftly and so tightly packed without colliding. When finally they settle down into breeding roosts, they are equally an astonishing sight. A single colony may cover fifty acres of bushveld and contain fifty million birds! The birds are sometimes also seen in Botswana and East Africa.

Related to the weaverbirds, the quelea is mostly pinkish brown, with the heavy bill of a seedeater. During the brood period—often timed perfectly to coincide with high insect population outbreaks—the parents gather enormous quantities of insects for their voracious young. Ornithologists report a thirteen-day incubation period with usually three eggs to a nest. The male builds the nest and then invites his mate to accept his cleverly constructed chamber—a beautifully woven spherical nest typical of weaverbirds everywhere.

During the breeding period nests are woven so close to one another in bushes and trees that the birds can scarcely maneuver between them.

Thomas Gilliard and Edmund Wolters reported having seen a colony of quelea with ten million nests. With three young in each nest, this would mean some thirty million open mouths to feed for sixteen days! At this time, the predators move in: snakes, several kinds of mongooses, and astonishing concentrations of birds of prey. Marabou storks, hawks, eagles, and a host of smaller raptors wheel in the skies above large quelea colonies and swoop down for a super feast.

Swarms of quelea do great damage to crops, especially during the period between broods, when the birds eat grass and weed seed and often descend onto fields of wheat, millet, sorghum, and rice. Irate farmers use explosives on roosting sites, killing hundreds of thousands of the birds. Yet they seem to make little dent in the total quelea population. However, the great bulk of the food of these birds is produced by nature in the wild savannahs and grassy steppes of eastern and southern Africa.

NATAL. This former province was South Africa's smallest, stretching from the southern borders of Mozambique and Swaziland to Transkei. Bounded in the east by the balmy, surf-washed Indian Ocean, and in the west by Transvaal, the Orange Free State, and Lesotho, Natal encompassed the territories colloquially known as Zululand, the traditional home of the Zulu people, which then numbered around seven million people. Peaceful and pastoral today, the Natal midlands were once the backdrop of clashes between the Britons, Boers, and Zulus. Many graves, forts, and museums are reminders of the conflict throughout the region.

Natal's scenic diversity included untamed wilderness, some with lush subtropical vegetation; broad, sandy beaches, coastal estuaries, and lagoons; plantations of sugarcane, eucalyptus, and pine; and the pinnacles of the Drakensberg Mountains. Holidaymakers basked in sparkling sunshine throughout the year. Durban, a thriving city of millions, is still one of the best, most modern resort complexes in Africa, if not the world. The city's port is the busiest in South Africa. Surf fishing, sailing, and surfing are extremely popular. From Durban, short drives north or south bring one to delightful resorts on a beautiful coastline.

The former Natal's two national game reserves, Umfolozi and Hluhluwe, recently were joined by a corridor and are noted for big game. It was in Umfolozi that much work was done to restore the endangered white rhino; both species of rhinos, white and black, have prospered so well as to allow gene pools and small breeding groups to be established in other parks.

Only one bridge spans the Umfolozi River to Hluhluwe. During a bad flood in the area a terrible tragedy occurred here. A ten-ton truck tried to negotiate the bridge with many park personnel aboard—many experienced members of the rhino capture team—and got swept downriver, drowning most of the workers.

Umfolozi and Hluhluwe combined encompass some three hundred thousand acres. The reserves feature many rhino of both species, plus nyala, zebra, impala, kudu, giraffe, and Cape buffalo. Some elephant are present as well as lion, leopard, hyena, and jackal. The cheetah is abundant. However, only one family of wild dogs presently can be seen in Hluhluwe. Bird life includes ostriches, and reptiles include the Nile crocodile and land terrapin.

Hluhluwe has magnificent scenery, with valleys, river bottoms, bushveld, and high escarpments. A beautifully designed lodge called Hill-top Camp has accommodations for about forty people, commands spectacular views, and serves excellent meals. There are also overnight accommodations outside the reserve, in nearby private lodges and camps.

The most famous mountains in the former province are the Drakensberg range, some within the province itself and some in neighboring Lesotho. The mountains are close to the Golden Gate Highlands National Park in the former Orange Free State (see above). They include meandering river valleys with trout streams, sparsely vegetated hills, high grassy ridges, many rocky overhanging cliffs, and stupendous barren mountaintops, some with such picturesque names as Rhino Peak and Giant's Castle. In one isolated valley, around seven thousand feet above sea level, a magnificent lodge, the Drakensberg Valley Inn, suddenly greets the visitor. The facility has *rondavels,* cottages, chalets, a swimming pool, dining facilities, and a golf course. There are a number of similar lodges. Eland and other antelope still can be seen in this high valley. In the evening sacred ibis take off from marshes and water holes and, like geese, fly in V formations, honking, headed for night abodes farther south in the valley.

In a second picturesque valley nearby there are additional facilities, including the Sani Pass Hotel, where four-wheel-drive vehicles with driver-guides can be hired for a mountain trip to Sani Pass. When I was there, the road up the pass, traversing the Drakensberg into Lesotho, was a somewhat hair-raising excursion distinguished by rocks, switchbacks, and hairpin turns. We seemed to hit more holes in a mile of gravel road than there were hairs on our heads. Starting in a lower valley where trees gave way to protea shrubs and then to grassy hillsides, the road got rougher and

fig. 27. A nyala antelope ram at a water hole in Mkuzi, South Africa.

ever more treacherous. At the boundary of Lesotho, an enclave country, where passports were
examined, the road grew even worse. The climb
was back and forth, one switchback after another,
up and up. When at last we reached the top of
Sani Pass, the saddle was level, windy, and cold,
with tundra conditions all around. A number of
small roundish huts made of stones and mud
suggested the bleak environment of faraway Ti-
bet. From a rough chalet on a picturesque promontory, we looked down into the deep canyon
below. Lesotho is locally known as the "roof of
Africa." Sani reaches ten thousand feet, but the

highest points in the Drakensberg are more than
a thousand feet higher yet. Snow is common in
the area and some skiing is available.

Sani Pass is home to the lammergeyer, and black
eagles nest on the cliffs. There are many caves,
some with Bushman paintings, indicating that
these people occupied the area before the eland
were killed off. Going down Sani Pass, the road
trip was easier but no less bumpy. In the lower
canyon reaches eland and other antelope may be
spotted.

The area that was Natal has many local nature
preserves, including St. Lucia on the coast, where

an estuary features many wallowing hippos and sunning Nile crocodiles. Hiking trails are numerous, as are picnic spots. The former Natal Parks Board did an outstanding job of preserving natural areas and developing facilities for outdoor recreation.

CAPE PROVINCE. Not only was this former province the largest in the country but it was also the nation's great scenic and floral kingdom. Much of the popularity of this region was due to the beautiful city of Cape Town, which is sandwiched between the sea and the mountains, at the foot of Table Mountain. A comely, sprawling city, it has long been the nation's legislative headquarters. Pretoria has been South Africa's administrative capital and its main business center. The area that was Cape Province has a great many provincial parks and preserves and numerous nature centers. A number of national parks are also spread over the former province.

In addition to a hoist to the top of Table Mountain (elevation nearly four thousand feet above sea level), Cape Town and its suburbs have many overlooks, gardens, and preserves. The waterfront development is a tourist attraction with scenic water views and a busy port. Once a year in September a wildflower festival is held at a central coliseum. The city's dam and reservoir in the nearby mountains feature a botanical garden, with the dam's spillway as a beautiful backdrop. Picnicking facilities and rondavels are available. A forestry park in the hills is also popular with visitors.

Near the city is Cape Point Nature Reserve, a 4,700-acre park that occupies Cape of Good Hope. Here the southernmost tip of Africa meets the sea, creating a three-ocean shoal (Indian, Antarctic, and Atlantic) that sends plumes of

white water shooting into the sky. First in beauty and second in violence only to Cape Horn in South America, it is an extraordinary and memorable spectacle.

At the Cape Point reserve, game animals wander undisturbed by predators, and food and water are plentiful. The chacma baboon is a frequent sight, as are giraffe, zebra, springbok, eland, wildebeest, and other antelope. Ostriches romp over the landscape and many larks, doves, and weaverbirds can be seen. The rock hyrax or dassie often is heard squeaking from rocky ledges. At the Cape Point parking lot and overlook are an information booth, a gift shop, and restrooms.

For the adventurous, a hillside walk of some five hundred feet leads to a sheltered overlook with a commanding view of the shoals, their roar clearly audible. Here is where Africa ends, as does this overview of a glorious continent and its many wild edens.

One of the fascinating points of interest not far from Cape Town is the Boulders area where, of all things, a colony of jackass penguins can be seen sunning along seaside rocks and calling out in nesting coverts. It is said that, when the Portuguese navigator, Vasco Da Gama, went ashore near the picturesque Cape of Good Hope, he noted large black and white flightless birds on one rocky shore. They were fascinating to watch, he reported, and brayed loudly like asses—hence their name.

In Addo Elephant National Park north of Port Elizabeth, the densely vegetated natural habitat supports around two hundred elephants, plus rhino, buffalo, eland, red hartebeest, and kudu. Over 170 bird species occur in the park. Night drives are offered on request. Accommodations and a restaurant are available.

Farther north, just west of Cradock, lies the

fig. 28. *A warthog with prized tusks and prominent warts below the eye.*

Mountain Zebra National Park, established to ensure the survival of the rare mountain zebra. The park is home also to a variety of other game. Still farther north in the semiarid plateau country is the Karoo National Park, noted for its unique karoo flora and well-stocked game.

Around Upington, along the Orange River, a profusion of vineyards and citrus groves adorn the river valley, attracting many birds. Around Calvinia in August and September the spring wildflowers herald the beginning of Namaqualand, stretching to the south. The region around Clanwilliam and Springbok then becomes a wildflower paradise—a scene unlike any other floral display. Here daisies, vygies (Mesembryanthemum), a type of yellow sunflower, ice plants, and some five hundred other indigenous wildflowers form an eden of floral design and extent almost impossible to describe. If spring rains come, Namaqualand becomes a wildflower spectacle second to none on earth.

Heading south from Clanwilliam one comes to Langebaan Lagoon in the West Coast Provincial National Park, said to be the longest salt- and brackish-water lagoon in the world. Whales have returned to the lagoon; the whale station has long been closed. Many eland and springbok can be seen in the park as well as great concentrations of waterbirds in the marshes and on the mudflats.

At Lambert's Bay, at a fish processing station, a rocky peninsula supports hundreds of nesting cormorants in September. And nearby, a seaside concrete boardwalk leads to Bird Island, a sandy and rocky island that is taken over by fourteen thousand nesting and noisy gannets. The island, several acres in extent, is jammed with exposed nests, squawking birds, and beating wings.

The Kalahari Gemsbok National Park—which is made up of two sections, one here in the former Cape Province, the other in Botswana—is another premier national park, though not as heavily visited as some of the others because of the great distances involved in getting there. The southern

entrance gate to the park at Twee Rivieren is situated two hundred miles north of Upington. The Kalahari Gemsbok National Park in this former province occupies a finger of the Northern Cape between Namibia and Botswana. Its size is 3,700 square miles—roughly half that of the Kruger National Park—but when taken together with the adjoining Botswana park, the total area of the two Kalahari parks is a staggering 79,000 square miles, larger than the state of Oklahoma.

This is the largest nature conservation area in southern Africa and one of the largest unspoiled ecosystems in the world. There is no fence between the two parks, and animals roam freely in response to seasonal changes—rainfall and the prevailing grazing conditions. At times they trek in the thousands across the plains. Against a background of rust-red sand dunes and wide horizons, the game is easily seen. It is here where the famed

fig. 29. Young elephants sparring.

black-maned lion can still be found. This is not a separate species of lion but simply a variation of the common form, *Panthera leo,* which occurs in many parts of Africa. The darker mane and heavier weight may be due to the colder climate away from the equator.

Despite the harsh environment of the Kalahari Gemsbok park, marked by low, rolling, unstable sand dunes, bird life is remarkable in species as well as numbers. As expected, sand grouse are most common, large flocks coming to drink at the pans and water holes following brief rainstorms. Present also is the thoroughly confusing but numerically rich list of passerine birds, which includes the sunbirds, starlings, buntings, pipits, and larks. Where the reserve displays old dry watercourses with bordering stands of camelthorn acacia, one can see the perpetually active nests of the social weavers, plus many lovebirds and finches. Small owls, namely the pearl-spotted and the scops, are heard at night. By day the large raptors, such as the chanting goshawk, other hawks, and eagles, are frequently sighted. Two large diurnal birds frequently seen in the savannah grasses are the regally strutting secretary bird and the kori bustard. Both, however, are shy, solitary birds, not easily approached. Getting close to them requires skilled stalking.

The landscape of the park is characterized mainly by rolling Kalahari duneland with scattered grasses, bushes, and hardy trees. Camelthorn trees and other species of acacia line the dry beds of two rivers, the Nossob and the Auob, which are prominent features of the park. Both watercourses originate east of Windhoek in central Namibia, and they join at the southern tip of the park. The word *river* is misleading, as the Auob remains dry for years at a stretch and the Nossob flows perhaps once a century. Yet underground flow persists along their courses, supporting the big trees, and in the microclimate provided by their shade, significant other plant life can survive.

Thus, these watercourses cover less than 1 percent of the park area, but the greatest concentrations of wildlife are found along them. Today, there are about eighty windmills with dams and watering holes along the riverbeds and on the dunes between them. Blue wildebeest, hartebeest, and springbok gather here to drink and in turn attract a variety of predators. Gemsbok are very common. In September the wild tsama melon, the size of a small grapefruit, can be seen here and there. It is the fruit of a low vine and helps quench the thirst of many animals and wandering Bushmen. Wild cucumbers and monkey oranges also can be seen.

Kalahari Gemsbok National Park is the kind of place that is so far from all else, such a rarefied experience in the desert, that almost no one goes there on a first trip to Africa, when most visitors are more concerned with seeing profusion and going to the "big ticket" parks; it's the kind of place one gets curious about after having seen the others.

The feeling one gets upon completing their tour of the parks of South Africa is that of both exhilaration and nostalgia—the joy of having been enriched by a beautiful and bountiful world but the reluctance of the mind and heart to say adieu. But there is tomorrow and hope. To return once more to Africa? Perhaps. If not, then surely to return again and again in one's dreams.

Appendix 1

DAVID LIVINGSTONE AND THE WILDERNESS HE LOVED

David Livingstone was the man who shed more light on the mysterious and forbidding Central African wilderness than anyone else who ever lived. Up until as recently as the 1850s, the great bulk of Africa south of the Sahara, barring a developing fringe of coastal southern Africa, was one big question mark as far as the people of Europe were concerned. It remained for explorers like Livingstone, Stanley, Burton, Speke, and others to change all that. After that, changes came rapidly.

Today our world changes almost too fast for comfort. Instant communication is here. With the press of a button directing an orbiting satellite, one can peer down and inspect almost every acre of the earth's surface. Thus armed with intensive geographical detail illustrating the extent and giving insight into the terrain of his travels, one can see David Livingstone's incredible three journeys—encompassing a million square miles and spanning the greater part of his sixty-three years—as much more remarkable than they seemed even to his contemporaries.

The nucleus of interest in Central Africa for Livingstone—although his interests and travels were much wider—gravitated toward the upper Zambezi River and Victoria Falls, exciting places to which he returned again and again to renew his spirit. The magnet to Livingstone's heart and soul was the wilderness that now includes the edenlike enclaves of today's Chobe National Park and Moremi Wildlife Reserve in Botswana, Zimbabwe's Hwange and Victoria Falls National Parks, the Luangwa Valley and Bangweulu Swamp in Zambia, the Lualaba River and headwaters of the Zambezi at the Zambia-Zaire border, and Lake Tanganyika.

For a better perspective on the man who reconnoitered the vast region, a brief review of the famed explorer's background is in order. David Livingstone was born in poverty in Blantyre, Scotland, on March 19, 1813. His mother was a lowlander and his father a highlander. As a boy he worked in sweatshops, saved his money, and acquired skills as a blacksmith, carpenter, and jack-of-all-trades. He attended Glasgow University and majored in medicine and theology, earning degrees in both at the age of twenty-seven. At the urgings of a missionary society he decided on a missionary career in China but went instead to Africa. Having taught himself Latin, Greek, and mathematics, and with his handyman skills, he was a perfect candidate for spreading the gospel in wild Africa. Thus in 1840 he sailed for Cape Town, then went on to Port Elizabeth and set out by ox-drawn wagon for the mission station of Kuruman, some seven hundred miles to the north, arriving there on July 31, 1841. This was in what was then called Bechuanaland, now in the northern Cape of South Africa.

Livingstone continually traveled north, exploring the desert and naming new mammals and birds. The San or Bushmen people showed him how to survive in the desert and where to find water holes. At one point some two thousand miles north of Kuruman, he was asked to clean out a nest of lions from a possible new mission station. He shot a big lion, which charged him and crushed his upper arm. His companions helped finish off the lion but the damage was done. Livingstone's upper arm would never properly heal; after that, the explorer had to learn how to shoot with his other hand. The injury became a positive point of identification when Livingstone's body was sent to England in 1873.

In 1844 he married Mary Moffat and started exploring the Kalahari Desert, mostly in the hope of establishing a new mission station north of Kuruman. In the interim he identified many plants and named no less than ninety-one new bird species. Five years after his marriage, he made a second attempt to cross the Kalahari and find Lake Ngami, which had never been seen by a white explorer. On this second trek he took his wife and children with him. His first daughter died in infancy. They had four other children, Robert, Agnes, Thomas, and Anna.

Livingstone was the first European to see Lake Ngami and so named the large lake, the circumference of which is about a hundred miles. This alkaline lake runs dry every several years. When it is full, hundreds of thousands of flamingos flock to it to feed on algae and copepods. Ngami lies just south of the present-day town of Maun in Botswana, near the edge of the huge Okavango Delta, a river of grass and islands where the waters are sweet and ever-flowing. Whether Livingstone ever reached the Okavango is not certain. He continued northward and eastward across game-filled woodlands, through what is now the Moremi reserve and on to the banks of the Chobe River.

The Chobe in Livingstone's day was impressive, as indeed it is even now. Game of every description abounds. Here the famed explorer-naturalist named two new antelope, the puku and the sitatunga, both semiaquatic in their habitat, although they are now distributed only further north, dislodged from the area by settlement. Here, in an area called Savuti adjoining Chobe National Park, the procession of big game is a wondrous sight—elephants coming to drink, buffalo churning up dust, zebra issuing their strange squealing bark, and lions being much in evidence, heard almost every night. Camping in the bush at Savuti, as the campfire was flickering its last, I was treated to hearing a lion roaring so loudly that the earth seemed to tremble beneath our sleeping bags. Again and again came his deep, guttural, staccato roar.

"Do you know what he's saying?" our guide inquired from deep within his sleeping bag.

"No," came the response. What?"

"Well, the Makololo says he is merely asserting his kingdom. He's saying, 'Whose land is this? Mine, mine. MINE, MINE!'" I wouldn't argue.

In August, 1851, Livingstone traveled, without his wife and children this time, still farther north along the Chobe River to the upper Zambezi, a fascinating trip, accompanied by a friend named Oswell. With a small group, they returned to Chobe, picked up his family, and on August 12, 1851, left for Cape Town eighteen hundred miles away. His mind was made up. He would send his

fig. 30. Zebras must drink every day, traveling many miles for water.

family to England while he returned once more to the Zambezi, and then he would trek westward to the Atlantic coast in Angola, retrace his steps back to the upper Zambezi, and follow it eastward.

It was then that he discovered Victoria Falls and named the spectacular cataract after Queen Victoria. On the south bank of the river were a number of huge baobab trees; on one of them Livingstone carved his initials, still visible today. The area, now Zimbabwe's Victoria Falls National Park, is replete with elephants, sable, buffalo, and kudu. This is the heartland of the Livingstone wilderness, and the overjoyed explorer, reluctant to leave, paused before pushing on down the river. Next he explored the terrain and tributaries en route to its mouth, six hundred miles to the east

in Mozambique. Here he rested, and then followed the coast northward to Zanzibar where he booked passage to England.

Thus Livingstone's first twelve years in Africa came to an end. Reunited in England with his wife and children, the now famous explorer was soon scheming again. Would he, could he, dare suggest a return to Africa? He would. In a fully directed, fully funded expedition, he would return to the mouth of the Zambezi and take his wife with him. His purpose was to explore the navigability of the lower Zambezi, reconnoiter the Shire Highlands and Lake Nyasa (now Lake Malawi), and return once more to his beloved Victoria Falls.

Soon after they entered the mouth of the

fig. 31. Zebras flee from danger, usually staying close together for safety. Stallions often try to protect the herd from the rear.

Zambezi aboard the *Lady Nyasa,* Mary Livingstone died of fever. Although devastated by the tragedy, Livingstone kept going. His ships got bogged down in the river and, later, even his smaller boats met impassable rapids. Still Livingstone was able to explore the Shire Highlands and the area around huge, deep Lake Nyasa—found in recent years to contain more species of fish than are known in any other lake. He also trekked up the Zambezi to Victoria Falls. But his honest reports were so discouraging when they were read in England that his expedition was recalled.

Livingstone sailed one of the ships some twenty-five hundred miles across the Indian Ocean to Bombay, sold it, and bought passage to

England. By now, however, he was so well known, the Zambezi expedition notwithstanding, that he was able to mount still another expedition to Africa, this time to solve once and for all the riddle of the Nile for the Royal Geographic Society. He received funds from various sources, including his books, and using most of his own money set sail for Zanzibar in August of 1865. He delivered his daughter Agnes to Paris for further schooling and went on to Cairo and Bombay, finally arriving in Zanzibar in January, 1866. He was aided by John Kirk, a British government official, and Livingstone himself was appointed Consul for Central Africa (without pay). With his faithful servants, Suzi and Chuma, who had accompanied him on some of his other exploits, plus some Arab servants and fifty porters, he began his final trek into the interior. This was March, 1866.

He ascended the Rovuma River (between modern Tanzania and Mozambique) as far as he could go and then struck off westward and southward on foot across the plains and kopjes of the central plateau. Rounding the south shore of Lake Nyasa, he then trekked northwestward into the wild lowlands between Lake Bangweulu and Lake Tanganyika, often meeting Arab slave traders and ivory-carrying safaris.

The explorer's progress was slow. He lost most of his mules and oxen and began to grow weary, although his health was still quite good except for troublesome hemorrhoids and occasional bouts with gastritis. He kept voluminous notes and read his Bible a great deal. But Livingstone's wanderings became more and more confused and his messages to Kirk and to England became less frequent. He did send letters back with Arab slave traders he met, but most of his mail never got to England. Finally his letters ceased completely and almost everyone thought he was dead. Everyone, that is, but James Gordon Bennet of the *New York Herald,* who believed he was alive. Bennet thought about sending his crack foreign journalist, Henry M. Stanley, to Africa to look for Living-

fig. 32. Wildebeest gather at a water hole. Courtesy South African Tourism Board

fig. 33. *The dominant female hyena controls clan movements. These doglike flesh eaters hunt in packs and are efficient killers.*
Courtesy South African Tourism Board

stone—but not until Stanley finished his assignments in Paris, Cairo, Jerusalem, the Crimean War zone, and India.

When Stanley returned from the Far East and there was still no word from Livingstone. Bennet, sensing a great opportunity for his newspaper to boost circulation, gave the order: "Henry, go find Livingstone, dead or alive. But find him! If dead, send me every evidence of his death." Accustomed to this kind of order, Stanley lost no time going to Zanzibar and outfitting a search expedition. He had attended the opening of the Suez Canal and had been to Persia and India, but this was different. This was a challenge of extraordinary magnitude and he jumped at it.

Who was this man, Stanley? That gifted writer and researcher of *The White Nile,* Alan Moorhead, gives us a clue (p. 125):

He was a man whose real name was not Stanley at all, but Rowlands, a Welshman who was an American, a soldier who was a sailor, and now a journalist who was leading an expedition into the center of Africa. Soon the world would know all about his picturesque background: the awful *Dickensian childhood in a workhouse in Wales, his arrival as a cabin boy at New Orleans, where he took the name and nationality of a kindly American who adopted him as a son, his soldiering in the Civil War, at first for the South and then for the North, his rejection by his squalid mother on his return to England, his adventures in the American Navy and in General Hancock's campaign against the Red Indians, and latterly as a journalist in the British campaign against the Emperor of Abyssinia. This was the career of a man of iron, an adventurer who was every bit as hard and ruthless as the world in which he lived. Professor Copeland remarks poignantly: "No other famous man of his time got so high from a start so low. No one who understands him forgets that. He never forgot it himself."*

So in March, 1871, Stanley took off after Livingstone, starting on the coast at Bagamoyo and marching west some five hundred miles to Tabora, continually picking up clues here and there of the lost missionary-doctor-explorer.

Meanwhile, Livingstone's wanderings near the Lualaba River, in what today is western Zambia

fig. 34. Ruins of the Sultan's palace, Zanzibar.

and which he thought had something to do with the Nile, exhausted him. Sick, nearly toothless, his medical chest lost or stolen, he came upon a terrible massacre of Africans by Arab slavers, an episode that made him think he was in hell. Some three hundred fifty to four hundred people had been shot or drowned in a great melee as hundreds tried to escape across a big river. The nightmare so unnerved the explorer that he asked his followers to struggle on with him to Ujiji, a small, peaceful fishing hamlet on the northeast coast of Lake Tanganyika. The cruelty of the slave trade continued to haunt Livingstone and he vowed to help end it. And it was in Ujiji under a mango tree that Stanley found him, emaciated, heartbroken, and half dead. The date was November 10, 1871. Stanley's supposed greeting, "Dr. Livingstone, I presume," was to enter the realm of cliché.

Livingstone donned his old cap and simply said, "Yes," advancing toward Stanley with an outstretched hand.

"Thank God, Doctor," Stanley was to have said, "I have been permitted to see you."

Livingstone was to have replied, "I am thankful that I am here to greet you." The meeting electrified the world. Stanley and Livingstone became close friends, walked and boated together, even jointly explored the shores of the big lake, where many chimpanzees came to the beach.

Stanley stayed three months, trying to persuade the famous explorer to accompany him to England. But Livingstone politely declined the offer, saying he had more work to do. The two then walked three hundred long miles to Tabora, Stanley leaving ample supplies for Livingstone there and at Ujiji, and promising more supplies and men for him at Tabora. In March, 1872, the two parted, never to see each other again.

Buoyed by Stanley's visit and with health improved, Livingstone stayed in Tabora five months, writing and praying. When at last fifty-seven porters arrived with supplies, he was jubilant. In a few days he was on the go once more. He headed for Ujiji, then crossed Lake Tanganyika once more and again pushed on toward the Lualaba and Lake Bangweulu. Here he was sure a river flowed into the big lake, flowed out, and was the true source of the Nile. But he was wrong. By the early spring of 1873, ill, feverish, and still bogged down in a great swamp, he grew sicker and weaker until he had to be carried in a litter. On April 30 he could go no more and was taken into a hut in a village ruled by Chief Chitambo. He was placed on a cot but was too weak by evening even to take tea. At 11 P.M. one of his servants looked in on him. He was in bed, praying. By the next bed check at 1:00 A.M. (May 1, 1873), Livingstone was dead. He had managed to crawl out of bed and get down onto his knees to pray, when his upper torso fell limp on the cot.

Thus ended the heartbeat of an incredible man, the life and career of a poor Scottish boy turned jack-of-all-trades; avid student; ordained minister; doctor of medicine; linguist; missionary; self-taught naturalist; astronomer; navigator; lover of God, humanity, and nature; preacher turned explorer—a man who failed to find the source of the Nile but inspired others to find it, who failed to put an end to the slave trade but helped to hasten its end, who through repeated forays on the Zambezi and elsewhere gave the world a new vision of a great continent and a new appreciation of the power and perseverance of the human spirit.

Livingstone's body was prepared for a last journey home in the village where he expired. His

fig. 35. Author and wife at the Livingstone-Stanley marker in Ujiji.

heart and viscera were removed, placed in a metal box, and buried under a tree; his body was crudely embalmed with salt and smoke, wrapped in a calico shroud, and placed in a carrier contrived of bark and sail material. The body was tied to a two-man carrying pole and transported by a small band of faithful followers, led by Suzi and Chuma, all the way to Tabora, then another 500 miles to the coast, and finally by ship to England. A notable funeral took place with Henry Stanley as one of the pallbearers, carrying Livingstone's body into London's Westminster Abbey, where it was laid to rest under a flat stone slab in the left-side main aisle. The slab reads: "Brought by faithful hands over land and sea, here rests David Livingstone, missionary, traveller, philanthropist, born March 19, 1813, at Blantyre, Lanarkshire, died May 1, 1873 at Chitambo's village, Ulala."

Stanley made two more expeditions to Africa, both astonishing achievements in their own right, including the exploration of the Congo River to its mouth and the circumnavigation of Lake Victoria. He was knighted and became a member of Parliament. A peak in the Mountains of the Moon was named for him. In some ways his exploratory achievements matched those of Livingstone, making the two the greatest explorers who ever entered Africa.

Appendix 2

NATIONAL PARKS, GAME PRESERVES, AND WILDLIFE SANCTUARIES IN EAST, CENTRAL, AND SOUTHERN AFRICA

The nations making up the eastern, central, and southern regions of Africa are to be commended for their vision in establishing many fine wildlife sanctuaries. These natural treasures represent not only a vital living heritage for their host countries but also an important natural resource for the rest of the world.

Organizations working on behalf of wildlife conservation in Africa include the African Wildlife Foundation (Washington, D.C.); Wildlife Conservation International (New York); the East African Wildlife Society (Nairobi, Kenya); the International Union for the Conservation of Nature and Natural Resources (Gland, Switzerland); the Martin and Osa Johnson Safari Museum (Chanute, Kansas); the National Audubon Society (New York); the National Geographic Society (Washington, D.C.); the National Wildlife Federation (Washington, D.C.); the South African Wildlife Society (Johannesburg, South Africa); the Wildlife Society (Washington, D.C.); and the World Wildlife Fund (Washington, D.C.).

The terms *park, reserve, preserve,* and *sanctuary* all connote wildlife protection. National parks generally follow the American concept of distinctive natural areas set aside to preserve some outstanding aspect of nature, such as forests, scenery, geological phenomena, or plant and animal life. As a rule, nothing can be collected in a national park, except that sport fishing may be permitted. In Africa, the prime attraction is big game, although there may be much other wildlife. A game preserve is usually an area with fewer restrictions than a national park, where wildlife is protected but certain human uses, such as cattle grazing, may be permitted; in some countries the term *conservation area* is similarly used. A wildlife sanctuary usually means a haven for wild mammals, birds, and other species, although protection of all wild creatures is implied.

These areas designated by different types of conservation status vary in size, types of restrictions, methods of management, accommodations available or allowed, and control and supervision employed. A number of parks exist in name only or are at present chiefly outlines on paper, for which future development, use, and staffing are contemplated. Moreover, the human encroachment permitted on these areas varies from country to country and sometimes from year to year. Hunting or game cropping may be permitted in one zone of a park one year and closed the next. Thus the visitor should be informed on the current rules in effect and then adhere to them.

For ease of reference, parks and reserves are here

listed alphabetically, by country. Not all reserves are listed.

BOTSWANA

Central Kalahari Game Reserve. Vast desert area in central Botswana, nearest to the capital city of Gaborone. No roads, only game tracks across the desert. All Kalahari game species are present, including many interesting birds, reptiles, and fishes. This is wild desert country and a safari guide is a must.

Chobe National Park. Lies in northern Botswana, a drive of an hour and a half from Victoria Falls in Zimbabwe. Chobe is an open-woodland ecosystem of 440 square miles, situated on the Chobe River, which borders Botswana, Zambia, and Zimbabwe. This was the favored stamping ground of David Livingstone and offers some of the largest concentrations of game to be seen in Africa. During the dry months, May to September, one can see huge herds of elephant, buffalo, zebra, antelope, and other wildlife. The habitats are a mixture of riverine flood grassland, open woodlands, acacia thickets, and fossil lake beds. Outstanding bird life.

Kalahari Gemsbok National Park. A huge 3,475-square-mile area in remote southwestern Botswana, adjoining a sister park in South Africa (see discussion of Kalahari Gemsbok National Park, South Africa, below). Huge herds of gemsbok and other antelope can be seen. Here one can still find the famous black-maned lion roaming free, undisturbed, together with lesser members of the cat family. An experienced guide is essential. Bird life

abounds. Game viewing and photographing with telephoto lenses are rewarding experiences.

Khutse Game Reserve. Adjoining the Central Kalahari Game Reserve, this is undeveloped, wild, uncharted. All desert wildlife, including numerous birds, are seen. Again, a guide is a must.

Mabuasehube. While not a park or reserve, this outstanding water wilderness of some 5,790 square miles, with scattered pockets of river Bushmen, teems with wildlife. Crystal-clear waterways with scattered islands and lagoons, bordered by waving stands of papyrus. Big game and small game abound.

Makgadikgadi Pans Game Reserve. Includes the vast Makgadikgadi Pan. It harbors gemsbok and springbok in large herds and great flocks of flamingos during the rainy season. Surrounding the pans are savannah habitats with clumps of palm trees. Herds of up to ten thousand wildebeest and zebra have been seen in one day.

Moremi Wildlife Reserve. A 695-square-mile unspoiled watery wilderness, an eden for birds and other wildlife; just north of Maun and within the famed Okavango Delta. Noted for flocks of heron, ibis, stork, crane, egret, Egyptian and spurwing geese, eagles, doves, quail, and passerine birds. Giraffe, antelope, hyena, and hippo abound. Crocodiles can be seen in the lagoons along with malachite kingfishers and other reed birds. Lion and zebra roam the larger islands. Photographically outstanding. Guides essential. Tsetse flies, however, abound.

ETHIOPIA

Awash National Park. A small plains park located some 135 miles east of Addis Ababa on the edge of the Rift Valley. Present are a variety of dry grassland game, including both and lesser kudu, Soemmering's gazelle and beisa oryx.

Omo National Park. Remote and undeveloped twelve-thousand-square-mile park in the southwestern region, characterized by a broad U-shaped river valley. Has considerable plains game. No accommodations and accessible only by air.

Rift Valley Lakes National Park. A small, undeveloped park some hundred fifty miles south of Addis Ababa on the Ethiopia-Kenya highway. This 355-square-mile park is noted for its two lakes, Shala and Abiata, which contain waterfowl during the migration period. In the months of January and February, masses of ducks and geese rest here. Also seen are flamingos, pelicans, and storks.

KENYA

Aberdare National Park. A 293-square-mile mountain rain forest park featuring the famous lodges Treetops and the Ark, where viewers can spend an afternoon and night observing game under floodlights from terraces. The power unit is underground so that quiet prevails. Animals often seen are elephant, rhino, baboon, Cape buffalo, reedbuck, and waterbuck, and sometimes hyena, bongo, giant forest hog, genet, warthog, and colobus monkey. The jump-off points are Outspan and the Aberdare Country Club. A few campsites are available in the high country, where elevations range from seven thousand to around thirteen feet above sea level.

Amboseli National Park. A flatland preserve of 1,259 square miles near the Tanzania border, some 150 miles south of Nairobi. Habitats include grassland, scrub, riverine forest, savannah, marshes, and a dry lake bed. On clear days Mount Kilimanjaro looms above the plain with its astonishing snow-covered summit. More than eighty forms of mammals are seen here, including the big five, many antelope, giraffe, warthog, baboon, hyena, and some 680 closely monitored elephants. Birds are plentiful. A variety of accommodations are available, including Amboseli Lodge, tent camps, and campsites.

Lake Nakuru National Park. A park recently enlarged and now newly fenced, outside Nakuru. This is primarily a bird sanctuary. Many flamingos congregate here, plus other waterbirds. Also seen are many waterbuck, buffalo, impala, reedbuck, and vervet monkeys; chiefly lakeshore habitat. One can drive around the lake. Recently rhino have been reintroduced. Good accommodations.

Marsabit National Park. A wild desert scrub park situated around four-thousand-foot Marsabit Mountain. Despite the scant vegetation, large elephants are to be found here, as well as the Grevy's zebra and beisa oryx. This is still an undeveloped, remote park, with almost no accommodations; one must camp. One can fly in or drive but special permission is needed from the Kenya Wildlife Service.

Masai Mara Game Preserve. This is Kenya's five-star game preserve and most popular tourist mecca because it is, in essence, the upper extension of the famed Serengeti ecosystem, which lies mostly in Tanzania. The seven-hundred-square-mile preserve is famous for its large herds of migrating wildebeest, Thomson's gazelle, topi, hartebeest, and zebra. Many lions are present. Cheetah, leopard, and hyena are also found. The elephant and Cape buffalo are common. A few rhino can be seen. Hippos are present in the Mara and larger rivers. Keekorok Lodge has excellent accommodations and there are several tented camps, plus new accommodations in the western sector. The preserve has numerous birds of prey.

Meru National Park. Situated northeast of Mount Kenya, this 366-square-mile park is worth a visit because of its mixed habitat, ranging from forest to riverine grasslands, scrub, and savannah. Here one can see the rare white rhino plus all the others of the big five, in addition to many other animal species. The park is quite isolated in the Northern Frontier District but accommodations are ample. Many species of birds are seen here.

Mount Elgon National Park. Located in the western region of Kenya, the park is essentially forested mountain habitat. From its slopes one can easily make out Lake Victoria, into which its streams flow. Mount Elgon is Kenya's second highest mountain, at 14,178 feet. The rare bongo is sometimes seen. The nearest town is Kitale, which lies 234 miles west of Nairobi.

Mount Kenya National Park. A large mountain rain forest park encompassing all of Mount Kenya above eleven thousand feet. One can drive to the Met Camp at ten thousand feet then hike up into the Teleki Valley at fourteen thousand feet and beyond. This is Kenya's highest mountain, rising over seventeen thousand feet. Glaciers are present year-round. Elephant and Cape buffalo are common and on occasion the bongo is seen in the bamboo forest. Good jump-off places are Mount Kenya Safari Club, Naro Moru Lodge, and Mountain Lodge.

Nairobi National Park. A small but recently enlarged and splendid game park of over one hundred square miles just outside Nairobi. It has plains game, lion, cheetah, baboon, and many birds—around 450 species have been recorded here. Nearby also is the "orphanage," a zoo that is well worth the visit.

Salt Lick Sanctuary. This is a private wildlife sanctuary south of Tsavo West, where a magnificent concrete structure has been constructed overlooking a water hole almost steadily besieged by a wide variety of animals, including herds of elephant; sometimes as many as sixty elephants can be seen at a time. Also lots of giraffe, zebra, and antelope are seen. The principle here is the same as at Tree-tops and the Ark, only the facilities are newer.

Buffalo Springs National Reserve—Samburu National Park. Small adjoining game preserves north of Mount Kenya in the Northern Frontier District, 214 miles from Nairobi. The area is semidesert with the Ewaso Ng'iro River flowing through it, making it ideal for elephant, warthog, baboon, giraffe, and two kinds of zebra (the Burchell's and the rarely seen Grevy's). Present, too, are the beautiful beisa oryx and the long-necked gerenuk. Some lions and leopards are found here and a great variety of bird life. Crocodiles are seen in the river. Samburu Game Lodge is rated excellent.

Shimba Hills Game Reserve. Only thirty miles from Mombasa, the port city on Kenya's east coast, the Shimba Hills form a striking hilly contrast to the flatlands of this region. This is the only place in Kenya where one can see the sable antelope with its magnificent backward-curving horns. Although facilities are limited, the game reserve is well worth a day's outing from Mombasa.

Tsavo National Park, East and West. A huge 8,034-square-mile area of mixed wooded and open country harboring the largest elephant herds and the most black rhinos in Kenya. Tsavo East has semiarid flatlands of thornscrub dotted with baobab. The Athi and Galana Rivers harbor many crocodiles. All dirt roads in the park north of the Galana are closed to the public. In Tsavo West a trip to see crystal-clear Mzima Springs is a must. Some seventy hippo cavort in the springs by day. An underwater glass enclosure reveals numerous fish, some crocodiles, and hippos walking on the pool bottom. Most East African wildlife can be seen here, although photography is difficult because of the cover. Elephant watching at the water hole below Mudanda Rock is especially popular. Buffalo, zebra, giraffe, and many species of antelope are present. Bird life is prolific, with at least sixty-six kinds of sparrow, finches, weavers, and many barbets, parrots, rollers, starlings, and twenty-four species of shrikes. There are several fine lodges and a few tented camps. Tsavo West also has some rugged forested hills. A five-star park.

Kasungu National Park. Located near the town of Kasungu in western Malawi, this is the country's largest park, featuring most of the same mammal and bird species seen in East Africa. Mixed habitats.

Lengwe National Park. In this small park in the far south one may see the rare nyala antelope from an elevated screened blind overlooking a water hole. The park is accessible by road from the city of Blantyre, with the Livingstone River and the falls by the same name on the way. Both features were named after David Livingstone, who explored much of this country. There are no accommodations.

Nyika National Park. A medium-sized park in northern Malawi, not far from the northwest shore of Lake Malawi. The major big game species are found here, plus many species of birds. Some accommodations can be found nearby. Malawi is a lovely small country but quite poor and has yet to develop its limited park system.

NAMIBIA

Etosha National Park. A flat six-thousand-square-mile park in northern Namibia, some three hundred miles north of Windhoek. It is all fenced and features large concentrations of elephant, zebra, impala (including the reintroduced black-faced impala), springbok, kudu, eland, hartebeest, and giraffe. Many ostriches and other birds are present, including concentrations of storks, and during the wet season, pelicans, flamingos, and other waterfowl. Some three hundred lions are present. The game scatters widely during the rainy season when the huge Etosha Pan fills up with rainwater. The

135
Parks,
Preserves,
Sanctuaries

best game viewing occurs when the animals concentrate around the water holes. Three excellent rest camps are present: Halali, Namutoni, and Okaukuejo.

Namib-Naukluft National Park. An immense dryland preserve—the largest in Africa—consisting of sand dunes, dry riverbeds, rocky hills, and mountains, with scattered ostrich, gemsbok, and the rare mountain zebra. Largely sandy and gravelly habitat with camelthorn acacias in the lowlands. This is the oldest, driest, most picturesque desert in the world, featuring even a petrified forest. A few campsites are available. Travelers must have their own supply of gasoline, food, water, and camping equipment.

Skeleton Coast Park. An extensive coastal preserve along the cold, rainless but fog-bound Atlantic beaches reaching forty miles inland. Great area. Very wild, isolated, and remote. A large rookery of Cape fur seals can be seen on a rocky coastal strip north of Swakopmund. Again visitors must bring their own water, gasoline, food, and camping gear.

Waterberg Park for Endangered Species. A one-hundred-thousand-acre high plateau preserve with surrounding red sandstone cliffs, virtually poacher-proof with only one government access road leading to the top, and this tightly controlled by rangers from the De la Bat rest camp at the foot of the southern cliffs. This is primarily a refuge for endangered species, such as both species of rhinos, roan, tsessebe, sable antelope, and others. Present are the rare Cape vulture, black eagle, and reintroduced mountain zebra, buffalo, and giraffe. Cheetah, leopard, hyena, and jackal are also

present but no lions. Waterberg is the largest wilderness park exclusively dedicated to the preservation of endangered African wildlife. A nature center is planned.

RWANDA

Kagera National Park. Located in northeastern Rwanda bordering Uganda and Tanzania, this 970-square-mile park is made up of valleys, grasslands, marshes, lakes, and some acacia savannahs harboring animals found in its neighboring countries.

SOUTH AFRICA

Addo Elephant National Park. A small park set aside to protect a remnant herd of Cape elephants.

Bontebok National Park. A park set aside to protect the rarest of African antelope, a species a little smaller than a topi. From a low of seventeen the herd has increased to nearly one thousand.

Kalahari Gemsbok National Park. A 3,456-square-mile park in northwestern South Africa that joins the larger park (by the same name) in southwestern Botswana (see discussion of Kalahari Gemsbok National Park, Botswana, above). This is semiarid to arid wild land with major game viewing at water holes along usually dry riverbeds. Surprisingly, however, many plains game animals are found here, including gemsbok, springbok, eland, hartebeest, wildebeest, and lion, leopard, and cheetah. Very hot in December and January. Limited accommodations in three rest camps.

Kruger National Park. This is one of Africa's oldest and most outstanding large parks, with good controls and effective management. Spanning a total of 7,340 square miles in the northeastern part of the country with mixed terrain, largely acacia woodlands, savannah, and scrub lands, it harbors many elephant, zebra, and seventeen species of antelope, including an estimated 180,000 impala, 1,000 lion, 700 leopard, and 300 cheetah. Large, excellent rest camps.

Mountain Zebra National Park. A small park established for the protection of a race of Burchell's zebra. Accommodations new and superb.

Other National Parks and Game Preserves. South Africa has many other established parks and game preserves, including some in private ownership. For more information, write to the Republic of South Africa, Game Department, Pretoria, S.A. Also write to the Tourist Board, Johannesburg, S.A.

TANZANIA

Arusha National Park. A popular mixed wetland and scrub park with heavy lakeside cover featuring hippo, buffalo, elephant, and the famous Lake Manyara tree-climbing lions. This small 123-square-mile park is well worth a visit. Bird life is prolific, including flamingos and pelicans. Here too one can see the pygmy mongoose around termite mounds. The lodge above Lake Manyara overlooks the lake and has excellent accommodations.

Mikum National Park. This is a small park well worth a day's trip out from Dar es Salaam, the country's capital at the coast.

Mount Kilimanjaro National Park. The upper part of Mount Kilimanjaro, Africa's highest and most impressive mountain (elevation 19,340 feet), has been set aside as a national park. When in Arusha, where Kilimanjaro International Airport is located, make inquiries.

Ngorongoro Crater Conservation Area. A popular 2,500-square-mile area encompassing a 10-mile wide, 2,500-foot-deep extinct volcanic crater where large concentrations of big game are to be found, including elephant, rhino, zebra, eland, wildebeest and other antelope, lion, cheetah, leopard, and hyena. The area lies close to the Serengeti National Park. Masai tribesmen graze their cattle here. Excellent accommodations and scenic views at the rim.

Olduvai Gorge. Chiefly of interest for geological and anthropological reasons, this area within the Serengeti ecosystem is where Louis and Mary Leakey made their great hominid discoveries.

Ruaha National Park. An undeveloped 4,600-square-mile park in Tanzania's south-central highlands. The Ruaha and the Njombe Rivers come together here and provide excellent habitat for big game, including Tanzania's largest elephant herds. Roan and sable antelope are found; many birds. Accommodations are limited.

Selous Game Reserve. A huge park near Dar es Salaam where the rare and beautiful sable antelope is to be found. Additional facilities are being planned. Well worth a day's outing.

Serengeti National Park. Africa's most famous park and big game area, covering a grassland region of

5,600 square miles. Virtually every form of big game is found here ranging from elephant and rhino to giraffe, Cape buffalo, and many species of antelope, especially wildebeest, Grant's and Thomson's gazelles, topi, and hartebeest. Large prides of lion and good populations of other predators are present. The zebra herds are among the largest in Africa. Ostrich and other birds are also plentiful. This is the classic savannah country of East Africa, interspersed with some riverine acacia habitats, marshes, lakes, scrub woodlands, and kopjes. The Seronera Lodge and Lobo Lodge have good accommodations.

Tarangire National Park. A small park with many elephants, baobab trees, and storks.

UGANDA

Kidepo Valley National Park. A dry, 486-square-mile park in northern Uganda near the Sudan border. Habitat is mountainous. Many antelope. An undeveloped park area at present.

Murchison Falls National Park. A beautiful park of 1,557 square miles along the Nile River, including Murchison Falls where the river plunges through a narrow gorge. Decimated under the Idi Amin regime and in the upheavals that ended it, the park's elephant, hippo, Cape buffalo, and crocodile are slowly making a comeback. Para Lodge on the bank of the Nile is a favorite with visitors. There are many Uganda kob, other antelope, zebra, and buffalo. Lions are present, as are leopard, hyena, jackal, and lesser predators. Picturesque red termite mounds are seen everywhere. This could be, once again, a fabulous game park.

Ruwenzori National Park. This is the former Queen Elizabeth National Park, basking in the shadows of the Mountains of the Moon. The banks of the Kazinga Channel, between Lakes George and Albert, are loaded with waterbirds, including ducks, geese, storks, and egrets and are the haunt of elephant, hippo, waterbuck, buffalo, and crocodile. Some accommodations are being restored. As at Murchison, the park's big game has suffered but is recovering. The 767-square-mile park needs to be enlarged and its facilities renovated, but its potential is great.

ZAIRE

Formerly the Belgian Congo, the country has several national parks in its eastern mountain region where the mountain gorilla can still be seen.

ZAMBIA

Kafue National Park. A huge 8,492-square-mile park that straddles the Kafue River. Mixed habitats harbor many forms of big game and their attendant predators. Roan and sable antelope are present. Some accommodations exist. There are over five hundred miles of viewing roads, also some walking trails.

Luangwa Valley Game Preserve. A large 4,760-square-mile game preserve where some controlled large and small game hunting is permitted. Many plains animals are present, including the rare Cookson's wildebeest.

Mwera Marsh Game Preserve. A game preserve of 1,444 square miles with mixed habitats.

Sumba Game Preserve. A 736-square-mile game preserve on the shores of Lake Tanganyika.

ZIMBABWE

Rhodes Matopos National Park. Primarily an archeological area, this two-hundred-square-mile park has some plains game and bird life. It is not far from Bulawayo.

Victoria Falls National Park. A small but scenic park on the northeastern bank of the Zambezi River at Victoria Falls. Excellent accommodations. Big game, including elephant and sable antelope in the upper part of the park. The David Livingstone Museum is in town 5 miles away.

Wanke National Park. A large 5,540-square-mile park some fifty miles south of Victoria Falls. Mostly scrubland habitat featuring elephant, tsessebe, eland, impala, roan, and sable antelope plus predators. Several rest camps and many good dirt roads for viewing game are available.

Appendix 3

GUIDELINES FOR AN AFRICAN SAFARI

As we move toward the twenty-first century, international jet travel is becoming more and more commonplace, and more Americans and Europeans are going to eastern and southern Africa to see firsthand the fabulous game lands and their incredible wildlife. Preparing for such a trip can be simple or complex depending on how one chooses to go about it, the time available, and costs of the safari. Having a good, experienced travel agent do most of the work is the simplest course to follow. At the other extreme, one can do all of the arranging oneself. A third option is to use some of the services of a travel agent and do the rest on one's own. Making most of the arrangements independently gives one a good measure of control over time spent, places selected, and expense. Needless to say, the more one can do on one's own, the further money goes. However, a good deal of homework is required.

For the first-time visitor or less experienced traveler, there is much to be said for prearranged tours, either for a larger group or for as few as two persons. For larger groups, several reputable organizations are now conducting tours to East Africa, among them the National Audubon Society and the Sierra Club. For smaller groups, such commercial organizations as Adventures International, Geo Expeditions, KLR International, Questers, and others can work out specific safari trips. Still others, like the American Museum of Natural History, offer in-depth natural history tours. Both the conservation organizations and the commercial operators usually have experienced naturalists as guides.

COST

For most people cost is a significant factor. Many are eager to take an African safari but feel that the expense may be prohibitive. Do not rule out such a journey, however, without investigating the cost of a self-arranged trip. Making one's own arrangements can cut all costs except airfare. For example, one can plan to find hotel accommodations upon arrival. International airports may have direct phone links to hotels and lodges or a tourist desk to help visitors secure accommodations. Hotels may provide van service from the airport. In towns, one can save on meals by choosing restaurants with care and on transportation by walking to places of interest rather than taking a taxi or minibus.

In Nairobi, Arusha, Dar es Salaam, Kigali, Kampala, Salisbury, Johannesburg, or Gaborone, one can shop around for the most reasonable land tours; most large cities have good, responsible tour operators. A self-arranged trip with some portions in a guided group can be a workable scheme. If, however, comfort, convenience, and preplanned arrangements have more appeal, it is better to pay to have some reliable organization set everything up.

LAND TRANSPORT

The ideal way to travel in Africa is to have your own rented vehicle with a driver-guide. A minibus with an open roof hatch is best for up to five people. This way each passenger can have a window seat. Crowding nine or ten people into a minibus to save on transportation costs can be unwise. The same holds true with four-wheel-drive Land Rovers or Land Cruisers. Four or five to a vehicle is enough.

What about renting and driving your own vehicle? It can be done, of course, but this is not recommended, especially if one is not familiar with the roads or road conditions. Breakdowns may be frequent if road conditions are poor. Driving on the left-hand side of the road adds complications and can be dangerous if one is unaccustomed to it. Accidents can be time consuming even if not serious. In many areas, too, signs are poor or nonexistent. It may cost almost as much to rent and drive a vehicle as to get an experienced driver-guide and a well-maintained vehicle. With a tour vehicle and driver, all the responsibility is on the tour organization, which can be a good feeling. Schedules, safety, and any problems arising as regards breakdown or gas supplies are left to the tour operator.

BEST TIME TO GO

The best time of the year for an African safari depends upon one's interests and destinations. Birders, for example, may wish to tie a visit to the arrival of the winter migrants from Europe. In East Africa, most months are good because one is close to the equator and temperatures do not vary widely from month to month. Elevation has a more pronounced effect. The rainy days of October and November usually bring light precipitation, with heavier rains in April and May. But even in the rainy season there can be clear days. From late June through September, weather may be clear but hazy, and sometimes conditions are dusty, which for a wildlife photographer can be a vexing problem.

For all-around game viewing in East Africa, probably January and February are the best months; the poorest months are from October to December and April and May, largely because of the rains and the poor—sometimes almost impassable—dirt roads.

In South Africa one is farther from the equator in subtropical or temperate zones and must prepare accordingly. August to October—spring through early summer—are good for most of South Africa. Some parks may close between December and late March. The Kalahari, for example, can be unbearably hot between October and January.

An important factor to keep in mind is elevation. In the high plateau country of East Africa, the climate is pleasant all year. But down along the coast it is hot and humid. In South Africa June through August can be chilly to cold, although snow is uncommon. Most travel guides include temperature details.

LUGGAGE, CLOTHES, FOOT GEAR

Luggage, clothing, and other supplies need to be kept to a minimum. A good rule is to pack all one feels likely to need and then cut the quantity roughly in half. For luggage, one good duffle bag about twenty-seven to thirty-six inches in length with a good top zipper is ideal for miscellaneous clothes, sweater, boots, and gifts. This bag should be of lightweight nylon material and have a hand grip as well as a shoulder strap. In addition, one medium-sized suitcase (perhaps a twenty-three-inch overnighter) should contain your neater, pressed clothes and personal needs; this can be carried aboard airliners or checked with the duffel bag. In Africa, airlines limit each passenger to two pieces of checked baggage with a combined total weight not exceeding forty-four pounds. The overnight case should have a lock. For carry-on luggage, take a lightweight, roomy shoulder bag with several compartments, which can be your camera bag. It should have a side pocket for documents. Wallet and passport, however, should be carried next to one's person, perhaps suspended from a strong thong around one's neck.

As for foot gear, much depends on how much hiking or walking is anticipated. If the itinerary calls for some walking, a good pair of water-repellent boots (rubber bottoms and 6-inch leather tops) is ideal. The old Maine hunting boot is unsurpassed as foot gear for hiking, bird watching, and coping with shallow water or mud. For air travel and for general use in town and in camp, a light pair of leather oxford shoes with a mocassin toe or athletic shoes are best. The soles should be composition, crepe, or rubber.

A long-sleeved khaki safari jacket, two pairs of khaki trousers or other cotton pants or jeans, and three or four shirts (two long- and one short-sleeved) with roomy pockets are recommended. A hat is a good idea, and a lightweight raincoat or poncho and swimsuit can be useful. For safari wear, take several pairs of wash-and-wear underclothing and socks.

For air travel and for meals in hotels and lodges, a sports jacket, slacks, and several sports shirts will come in handy. Because nights can be cold, a good lightweight wool sweater should go into the duffel bag. Also throw in a large handkerchief useful as a dust mask when traveling over dusty roads. For toilet articles, carry only lightweight items—no big cans or bottles. Extra laundry soap and toilet paper are advisable; and take a spare pair of sunglasses.

OTHER GEAR
AND CAMERA EQUIPMENT

Although a canteen for water is not really needed, it can come in handy, as can water purification tablets. Other miscellaneous items often useful are a small flashlight with extra batteries, a pocket knife, and a sewing kit with extra needles, safety pins, and buttons. Take a small first-aid kit, anti-malaria pills, insect repellent, sunscreen, and aspirin.

For game viewing and bird watching a pair of center-focus binoculars is a must—7 × 35 glasses are good although eight or even ten power serve one even better. Anglers should bring their own fishing gear.

Photographic equipment and accessories can get involved, but for the amateur a good single lens reflex, preferably with both automatic and manual controls, is best. A wide-angle lens and a telephoto lens of up to about 300 mm are recommended. Haze filters, lens shade, and lens covers are needed. A unipod or a chestpod eliminates much camera shake. Serious amateur photographers may want to include a separate light meter and a backup camera. Sturdy plastic bags can help protect cameras from dust; lens cleaning paper, a lens brush, and rubber bands and scotch tape are handy also.

As for film, the main thing is to take plenty of it with you. Carry it in a cardboard or cigar box in your duffel and check it. *Do not* let the security people x-ray film, no matter what they say. If carrying film on one's person or in a shoulder bag, politely ask that these be separately checked.

Although many speeds of film are now available, the standard ASA 64 Kodachrome or Ektachrome produces good results in color transparencies. African weather is such that there is usually sufficient light for ordinary film. For color prints, high speed (ASA 400) film such as Koda-

color is adequate for automatic exposure shots and for indoor use without flash.

Those with larger format cameras should have both a standard 50 mm lens and a 250 mm telephoto, along with a double lens reflex camera as a backup. A unipod here is a must, and again be sure to bring all the film needed. Professional film may be hard to get and all film is expensive outside the United States.

Lastly, a word should be said about photographing people. In many countries people prefer not to have their picture taken without permission. Often they may negotiate for a small fee. Be sure *always* to ask permission before taking a picture. Also consider the other travelers when taking photos. Courteous conduct to everyone should be the rule.

Index

Note: Pages with illustrations are indicated by italics.

aardvarks and aardwolves, 86–87

Abdin's stork, 102

Aberdare Country Club, 27

Aberdare highlands, 6, 66

Aberdare National Park, 26–32, 133

Aberdare Range, as rainforest refuge, 25

Abyssinian monkey, 28

acacia trees, 17, 44, 45, 99, 101, 105

Adamson, George, 70

Adamson, Joy, 70

Addo Elephant National Park, 116, 136

Africa, preservation of, xiii–xv

African Wildlife Foundation, 14

Akeley, Carl, 9, 80

Albert, Lake, 7, 35, 37, 68, 82

Amboseli National Park, 3–5, 13–15, 133

American Museum of Natural History, 80

Amin, Idi, 88

Anderson, Charles, 101

antelope, *112, 115;* Aberdare, 27, 29; ancient, 55–56; Kalahari, 93, 94; Lake Manyara, 58; Meru, 73; Mount Kenya, 32; Namibia, 100, 102, 103, 105; Ngorongoro, 59, 61; Okavango, 94–95; Rift Valley lakes, 36, 37, 38; Ruwenzori, 81; Salt Lick, 15; Samburu, 66–67; Serengeti, 44, 47, 49, 52; South Africa, 111, 112–13, 114, 116, 119; Victoria Falls, 123. *See also* wildebeest

anthrax, 73, 102

anthropology, ancestral humans, 55–56

ants, dune, 106

apes. *See* baboons; gorillas, mountain

aphrodisiac, rhino horn as, 75–76

Ark Lodge, 26, 27, *28,* 29–32

Arusha National Park, 137

Athi River, 16, 17

Auob River, 119

australopithecine, 56

avifauna ecosystem, 35

avocets, 39

Awash National Park, 133

Baboona, 10

baboons: Aberdare, 27, 29; Lake Manyara, 58; Lake Nakuru, 37, 38; Meru, 73; Namibia, 100, 102; Serengeti, 44; South Africa, 116; Tsavo, 15, 17

Baker, Samuel, 67–68, 82

Banweulu, Lake, 128

baobab trees, 17, 19, 123

bateleur eagle, 32

Batian Peak, 32

bats, 79–80

bearded vulture, 56, 112, 115

bee-eater, 95, 113

beisa oryx, 66–67

Bennet, James Gordon, 125–26

Bernhard, Prince of Holland, 38

Berry, H., 104

biomass analysis in wildlife management, 21

Bird Island, 118

birdlife: Aberdare, 27, 29; feeding bonus from fires, 49; Kalahari, 92–93; Manyara Lake, 56; Meru, 70, 71–72; Mount Kenya, 32; Namibia, 100–101, 102; Okavango, 95; Rift Valley lakes, 35–41; Ruwenzori, 81; Samburu, 69–70; Serengeti, 44, 46–47, 49, 51; South Africa, 112, 113, 114, 115, 116, 118, 119; Tsavo, 17. *See also* eagles; waterfowl

black eagles, 100, 101, 112, 115

black-faced impala, 102

black korhaan, 102

black mamba, 100

black-maned lions, 119

black rhinoceros, 74, 102

blackthorn acacias, 101

black vulture, 46

black wildebeest, 112–13

boat transportation, 95, 96
Boer War, 109–10
Bogoria, Lake, 35, 36–37
bongo antelope, 32
Bontebok National Park, 136
boomslang snake, 100
Boringo, Lake, 35, 40–41
Born Free (Adamson), 70–71
Botswana, 39, 92, 132
Boulders area of Cape Town, 116
brood parasites, 72
Brown, Leslie, 39
brown hyena, 93, 100
Bruce, James, 9
Buenavelo, Lake, 39
buffalo, Cape. *See* Cape buffalo
Buffalo Springs National Reserve, 65–70, 134–35
Buganda. *See* Uganda
bullfrogs, 69
Burchell's zebra, 44, *50, 67*
Burton, Sir Richard, 9
bushbuck (antelope), 27, 29
Bushmen, Kalahari, 94, 115

caleocothere, 56
camel thorn tree, 105
camera equipment for safari, 143–44
camping: Aberdare, 27, 29, 32; Kalahari, 95; Lake Boringo,
    40; Lake Nakuru, 37–38; Namibia, 101, 102, 105;
    Serengeti, 49, 50, 102; South Africa, 114
candelabra tree, 38
Cape buffalo: Aberdare, 27, 29, *30,* 30–31; Lake Manyara, 58;
    Lake Nakuru, 38; Meru, 72; Mount Kenya, 32;
    Ngorongoro, 60–61; Ruwenzori, 81; Serengeti, 43, 49–
    50, 52; South Africa, 111, 114; Tsavo, 15, 17, 19; Victoria
    Falls, 123; Waterberg Park, 100
Cape Cross, Namibia, 104
Cape fur seals, 104, 106
Cape hunting dogs, 69, *71*
Cape of Good Hope, 9, 116
Cape Point Nature Reserve, 116
Cape Province, 116–19
Cape Town, South Africa, 116
Cape vultures, 100–101
carmine bee-eater, 95
Carstens, Vern, 10
cattle herding, 9

caves, Natal, 115
Central Kalahari Game Reserve, 93–94, 132
ceremonial daggers, rhino horn for, 76
chacma baboon, 116
Chagga people, 8, 9
Chania Falls, 27
cheetahs: Namibia, 100, 102; Ngorongoro Crater, 61–63, *62;*
    Ruwenzori, 81, *87;* Serengeti, 48; South Africa, 114;
    Tsavo, 17
Chitwan National Park, 76
Chobe National Park, 122, 132
Chobe River, 122
clapper larks, 102
Clapperton, Hugh, 9
clear-cut logging, 25
climate, 8, 25, 143
climbing and hiking, 5–7, 27, 32–33, 116
clothing recommendations, 143
colobus monkey, 27–28, 29
cormorants, 36
Congo basin, wildlife losses in, 25
Congorilla, 10
conservation, wildlife: and grazing in Kalahari, 92; need for
    African, xiii–xv, 28; organizational resources, 131; rhino
    preservation in Natal, 114; static vs. dynamic, 21. *See also*
    endangerment of wildlife
conservation area, definition, 131
Cookson's wildebeest, 138
coots, 17, 29, 39, 58, 95
cormorants, 118
costs of safari trips, 141–42
cranes, 44
crimson-breasted shrike, 100, 102
crocodiles, Nile: Ruwenzori, 81, 82; Samburu, 67–69;
    Serengeti, 51; South Africa, 114, 116; Tsavo, 17
culling of elephants, 110–11

da Gama, Vasco, 9
Damara dik-dik, 102
Dart, Raymond, 56
dassies, 6
date trees, 102–103
De la Bat camp, 101
Demara people, 101
Demara Region of Namibia, 103
desert habitat, 91–96, 99, 118–19, 122
dik-diks, 102

Dinesen, Izak, 4
dinosaur evidence, 101
dinotherium, 56
disease epidemics, animal, 73, 102
dogs, wild, 47–48, 69, *71*, 102, 114
donga, 55
doves, 44, 46, 100, 102, 113
Drakensberg Mountains, 112, 114
Drakensberg Valley Inn, 114
drama, wildlife, 29–32
drought, 17, 19–20
ducks: Aberdare, 29; Lake Manyara, 58; Lake Nakuru, 39; Okavango, 95; Samburu, 69; Tsavo, 17
Durban, South Africa, 114

eagles: Kilimanjaro, 6; Manyara Lake, 58; Mount Kenya, 32; Namibia, 100, 101, 102; Okavango, 95; Rift Valley lakes, 37, 41; Samburu, 69; Serengeti, 46; South Africa, 112, 113, 115; Tsavo, 17
ecological zones of Kilimanjaro, 5
egrets, 39, 44, 95
eland: Namibia, 102; Ngorongoro, 59, 61; Serengeti, 44; South Africa, 112, 114, 116
elephants: Aberdare, 27, 29, 31; Cape Province, 118; endangerment of, 88; Kitum Cave, 79; Manyara Lake, 57, 58; Meru, 72; Mount Kenya, 32; Namibia, 102, 106; Okavango, 95; Ruwenzori, 81, 82; Samburu, 65–66; Serengeti, 43, 52; South Africa, 110, 111, 114; Tsavo, 13–23, *16, 18, 20, 22;* Victoria Falls, 123
Elgon, Mount, 79
Elizabeth, Queen of England, 26
endangerment of wildlife: Congo basin, 25; elephants, 88; gorillas, 88–89; Nile crocodile, 68; rhinoceros, 74–77, 114; wild dogs, 69, *71*
Ethiopia, 46, 133
ethnic mix in South Africa, 110
Etosha National Park, 99, 101–103, 135–36
Etosha salt pan, 39
European exploration of Africa, 9, 41, 93, 121–30
Ewaso Ng'iro River, 66, 68

fairy shrimp, 45
farming, 9, 25
fever trees, 45
fig trees, 95, 101, 102–103
fires, grassland, 49
fish eagles, 17, 41, 58, 95

fishes: kingfish, 104; in Lake Malawi, 41; lungfish, 69; perch, Nile, 82, *84;* rock bass, 104; and soda lakes, 37; tilapia fish, 17, 41
fishing, Skeleton Coast, 103–104
Fish River Canyon, 99
Flame Trees of Thika, The (Huxley), 4, 26
flamingos: ancient, 56; Kalahari, 93; Okavango, 95; Rift Valley lakes, 35, 36–37, 39; Serengeti, 46
foot gear recommendations, 143
foot safari, Meru, 72
foot trails, at Aberdare, 27. *See also* hiking
forested habitat, 5, 25–33, 59, 70–77
Fossey, Dian, 88–89
fossils, Namibian Petrified Forest, 103
francolin, 101, 102
Freddie, King of Uganda, 88
fur seals, Cape, 104, 106

Galton, Sir Francis, 101
game preserve, definition, 131
game wardens, 19
gazelles: Manyara Lake, 56; Ngorongoro, 61; Samburu, 66; Serengeti, 44, 47, 49, 52. *See also* springbok
gear for safari trip, 142–44
geese, 46, 58, 82, 95
gemsbok: Kalahari, 93, 94; Namibia, 100, 102, 103, 105; South Africa, 119
genets, 27
geographic features, overview of African, 8. *See also* desert habitat; great plains; lakes; mountains
geology of Waterberg Park, 101
George, Lake, 7, 35, 37
German influence in Namibia, 99, 101
giant forest hog, 27, 29, *30*
giant strangler fig tree, 95
Gilliard, Thomas, 113
Gilman's Point, 6
giraffe-gazelle, 66
giraffes: Aberdare, 27; Lake Manyara, 58; Meru, 72–73; Namibia, 100, 102; Ruwenzori, 81; Serengeti, 44, 49, 52; South Africa, 111, 114, 116; Tsavo, 15, 17
glaciers, 134
Golden Gate Highlands National Park, 112
gorillas, mountain, 80, 88–89, 138
goshawk, 102, 119
Governor's Camp, 49, 50
Grant's gazelle, 44, 47, 61

grasslands. *See* great plains
Great Britain, handling of Uganda, 88
great plains: Kilimanjaro, 5–6; Namibian, 99–101, 102–103; Serengeti, 7, 43–52; Tsavo, 17, 19
Great Rift Valley: and Kilimanjaro, 4, 6; lakes of, 35–41, 133; northern section, 65–77; views of, 26
Grevy's zebra, 67, 73
grew rhebok, 112
griffin vultures, 51
ground hornbill, 44, 49, 58, 69
Grzimek, Bernard, 63
guides, value of, 58
guinea fowl, 46, 102
Guru Falls, 27

habitat analysis wildlife management, 21–22
Halali camp, 102
hamerkop, 70, 71–72
Hamilton, Ian Douglas, 57
Hardy, Ian, 29–32
Hargraves, Bruce, 92
hartebeest, 44, 94, 102, 119
Haunted Forest, Etosha, 103
hawks, 46, 69, 102, 113, 119
headstander beetles, 106
Hemingway, Ernest, 5
Hemingway Overlook, 5
Hennington, Lake, 37
Herero tribe, 101
herons: Aberdare, 29; Lake Manyara, 58; Lake Nakuru, 39; Okavango, 95; Samburu, 69; Tsavo, 17
Hewston, John, 106
high altitude rainforests, 3–10, 25–33
hiking, 5–7, 27, 32–33, 72, 116
Hilltop Camp, Natal, 114
hippopotami, *111;* Lake Boringo, 17; Lake Manyara, 58; Ruwenzori, 81–82; Serengeti, 51; South Africa, 116
historical views: European contact with Africa, 9, 41, 93, 121–30; from Kilimanjaro, 6; South Africa, 109–10; Uganda, 88
Hluhluwe game reserve, 114
hogs: giant forest, 27, 29, *30;* warthogs, 15, 17, 67, 94, 100, *117*
hominids, ancient, 55–56
honeyguide, 70, 71–72
hoof and mouth disease, 73
hook-lipped rhinoceros, 74, 102
hornbills, 44, 49, 58, 69, 100

Horombe Hut, 7
hotels. *See* lodging
hot springs, 37
humans, ancestral, 55–56
hunting styles, carnivore, 47–49
Huxley, Elspeth, 4
hyenas, 81, 93, 100, 102, 114. *See also* spotted hyena

ibis, sacred, 27
impala: Lake Manyara, 58; Lake Nakuru, 38; Namibia, 100, 102; Ruwenzori, 81; Serengeti, 49, 52; South Africa, 111, 112–13, 114
intelligence levels, elephants, 14
International Union for the Conservation of Nature, 76
Island Camp, Lake Boringo, 40
ivory, poaching for, 21

jacanas, 95
jackals, 102, 114
Johnson, Martin and Osa, 10, 19

Kafue National Park, 138
Kagera National Park, 136
Kalahari Desert, 91–96, 118–19, 122
Kalahari Gemsbok National Park, 93, 118–19, 132, 136
Karoo National Park, 117
Kasungu National Park, 135
Kazinga Channel, 81
Keekorok Lodge, 134
Kenya: attractions of north, 65–77; hominid excavations in, 56; lakes of, 35, 39; parks and reserves of, 133–35; and Serengeti, 43
Kenya, Mount, 5, 6, 25, 32–33, 65
Kenyatta, Jomo, 38
Khutse Game Reserve, 132
Kibo Lodge, 5
Kibo Peak, 5, 6, 7
Kidepo Valley National Park, 138
Kilagoni Lodge, 16
Kilimanjaro, Mount, 3–10, *4*
Kilimanjaro National Park, 5, 9
kingfish, 104
kingfisher, 17, 39, 58, 69–70, 95
Kirk, John, 124
kites, 35
Kitum Cave, 79–80
kokerboom tree, 99

kopjes (granite hills), 45
kori bustard, 35, 44, 49, 102, 119
Krapf, Ludwig, 5
Kruger National Park, 110–11, *111,* 136–37
Krutch, Joseph Wood, 91
kudu: Etosha, 102; Meru, 73; Salt Lick, 15; South Africa, 111, 114; Victoria Falls, 123; Waterberg Park, 100
Kunene River, 102
Kuruman, 9, 93
Kururu Falls, 27

Lake Borgoria Nature Reserve, 36
Lake Manyara Lodge, 57
Lake Manyara National Park, 55, 56–58
Lake Naivasha Hotel, 36
Lake Nakuru National Park, 38, 133
lakes: Manyara, 55, 56–58; Ngami, 93, 122; Nyasa/Malawi, 124, 125; Rift Valley, 35–41, 133; Ruwenzori area, 82; Samburu area, 68; Tsavo area, 19
Lambert's Bay, 118
lammergeyer, 56, 112, 115
Lander, Richard, 9
land terrapin, Natal, 114
Langebaan Lagoon, 117–18
larks, 102, 113
Leakey, Louis and Mary, 56
Leakey, Richard, 56
lechwe, 94–95
Lengwe National Park, 135
leopards: Aberdare, 27, 29; Lake Manyara, 57; Meru, 70, 72, 73–74, *74;* Mount Kenya, 32; Namibia, 100; Serengeti, 43, *44,* 45, 48; South Africa, 111, 114; Tsavo, 17
Lesatima, Mount, 26
Lesotho, 109, 115
lilac-breasted rollers, 102
Lion Hill Camp, 37–38
lions: Aberdare, 27, 29; Lake Manyara, 57–58; Meru, 72; Namibia, 102, 106; Ngorongoro, 60, 61; Ruwenzori, 81; Savuti area, 122; Serengeti, 43, 45–46, *46,* 47, *48,* 48–49; South Africa, 110, 111, 114, 119; Tsavo, 17
Lioto Hills, 50
Livingstone, David, *7,* 9, 41, 93, 121–30
Lobo Lodge, 138
lodging: Aberdare, 26–27, *28,* 29–32; Lake Manyara, 57; Masai-Mara, 134; Mount Kenya, 5, 32, 134; Namibia, 101; Ngorongoro, 59, 61; Ruwenzori, 81, 82; Salt Lick Sanctuary, 15, *16;* Samburu, 66, 68–69, 135; Serengeti,

49, 138; South Africa, 114; Tsavo, 16. *See also* camping
lowland rain forests, loss of African, 26
Lualaba River, 127–28
Luangwa Valley Game Preserve, 138
luggage recommendations, 142–43
lungfish, 69

Mabuasehube wilderness, 132
makalani palms, 102–103
Makgadikgadi Pans Game Reserve, 39, 92, 93–94, 132
malachite kingfisher, 95
Mala Mala game preserve, 111
malaria, 45
Malawi, Lake, 7, 35, 41, 124, 125
Malawi, parks and reserves of, 135
Manyara, Lake, 55, 56–58
manyattas, 9, 57, 60
marabou stork, 37, 39, 46, 113
Marangu Huts, 7
Mara River, 45, 49, 50–51
maroela, 102–103
Marsabit National Park, 19, 133
Martin, Esmond B., 76
Masai Mara Game Preserve, 43, 47, 134
Masai people, 8–9, 57, 59
Maun, Botswana, 94
Meru National Park, 6, 65, 70–77, 134
Met Camp, 32
Meyer, Hans, 5
microclimates, Mount Kenya, 32
migration, 22, 49, 50–51, 52
Mikum National Park, 137
missionary operations, historical, 9
Moffat, Mary, 122, 124
Moffat, Robert, 9
mokoro dugout, 96
Mombasa, Kenya, 6–7
mongooses, 27, 85, 101, 102, 113
monitor lizards, 85, 87
monkeys, 17, 27–28, 29, 37
Moorhead, Alan, 126–27
mopane, 102–103
Moreni Wildlife Reserve, 132
Moringa ovalifolia trees, 103
Mosquito Creek, Tanzania, 57
Moss, Cynthia, 14
Mountain Lodge, 32, 134

mountains: Aberdare Range, 25; Drakensberg, 112, 114; Kenya, 5, 6, 25, 32–33, 65; Kilimanjaro, 3–10, *4;* Lesatima, 26; Ruwenzori, 7, 8, 79–89; Table, 116; volcanic highlands, 26, 55–63
Mountains of the Moon, 7, 8, 79–89
mountain zebra, 103
Mountain Zebra National Park, 117, 137
Mount Elgon National Park, 134
Mount Kenya Safari Club, 32, 134
Mount Kilimanjaro National Park, 137
Mto wa Mhu, Tanzania, 57
Murchison Falls, 68, 82, *83*
Murchison Falls National Park, 82–89, 138
Mwenzie Peak, 7
Mwera Marsh Game Preserve, 138
Mweya Lodge, 81
mythology, of Kilimanjaro, 3, 8–9
Mzima Springs, 16, 17, 135

Nairobi, Kenya, 4, 6, 26
Nairobi National Park, 134
Naivasha, Lake, 35, 36
Nakuru, Lake, 35, 37–40
Namib Desert, 99
Namibia, 39, 99–106, 135–36
Namib-Naukluft National Park, 99, *100, 104, 105,* 105–106, 136
Namutoni camp, 102
Naro Moru Lodge, 32, 134
Natal region, 113–16
Natron, Lake, 39
Nelion Peak, 32
Ngami, Lake, 93, 122
Ngong Hills, 4, 26
Ngorongoro Crater, 37, 47, 52, 55, 58–63
Ngorongoro Crater Conservation Area, 43, 137
Ngorongoro Crater Lodge, 59
Ngorongoro Wildlife Lodge, 61
Niger River, 9
Nile crocodile. *See* crocodiles, Nile
Nile River, 9, 80–89, *83, 85,* 124–25
Nilotic peoples, 88
Nossob River, 119
nyala, Natal, 114, *115*
Nyasa, Lake, 7, 35, 41, 124, 125
Nyika National Park, 135

oasis. *See* waterholes

Obote, Milton, 88
okapi, 32
Okaukuejo camp, 102
Okavango Delta, 91, 92, 94–96, 132
Okavango River, 94
Olduvai Gorge, 55–56, 137
olive-backed baboons, 58
Omo National Park, 133
Orange Free State area, 110, 111–13
Orange River, 93, 110
oribi, 112
oryx, 66–67
ostriches: Kalahari, 92; Namibia, 102; Samburu, 69; Serengeti, 44, 46; South Africa, 116
Out of Africa (Dinesen), 4
Outspan transfer station, 27
owls, 35, 119

Paradise, Lake, 19
Para Lodge, 82
parks, summary of, 131–39. *See also individual park names*
pelicans, 39, 40–41, 58, 82
penguins, jackass, 116
perch, Nile, 82, *84*
Peterson, Roger Tory, 38–39, 72
Petrified Forest, Namibia, 103
photography, historical, 10
physiography, in Manyara Lake area, 57
pied crows, 44, 101, 113
plains, great. *See* great plains
plant life: Aberdare, 27; grasses, savannah, 45; Kilimanjaro, 6; Mount Kenya, 32; Namibian, 101, 102–103; Ngong Hills, 26; South African, 112, 113–14, 117; Tsavo, 17. *See also* trees
plovers, 95
poaching: devastation of, 17; of elephants, 14, 21; interdiction of, 19, 22; of rhinoceros, 76–77; Waterberg Park as protected from, 100
podocarpus trees, 79
poincianas, royal, 26
Pokot people, 65
politics, and safari safety, xv
Pool, Joyce, 14
population issues, and Tsavo drought, 20–21
powdered rhino horn, 75–76
preserves, game. *See* parks, summary of
primates. *See* baboons; gorillas, mountain; monkeys

private game preserves, 111, 112–13
protohumans, 56
provinces, South African, 110
Ptolemy, 80
puff adder, 100
Purtscheller, Ludwig, 5
pythons, 100

Queen Elizabeth National Park, 81–82
quelas, red-billed, 113
quiver tree, 99

railroad development, 6
rails, 29, 95
rainforests, 5, 25–33, 70, 79
rains, and rhythm of life, 45
raptors. See eagles; hawks
Redmann, Johannes, 5
reedbuck, 38, 94
religion, as source of political friction, 88
reserves, game. See parks, summary of
rhinoceros: at Aberdare, 27, 29; drought effects on, 19; en-
    dangerment of, 74–77; at Lake Manyara, 57; at Lake
    Nakuru, 38, 40; at Meru, 70, 74–75, 75; in Namibia,
    100, 102; at Ngorongoro, 59–60, 60; northern white, 6;
    preservation methods, 23; in Salt Lick Sanctuary, 15; in
    Serengeti, 43, 52; in South Africa, 111, 112–13, 114; at
    Tsavo, 17
Rhodes Matopos National Park, 139
Rift Valley, Great. See Great Rift Valley
Rift Valley Lakes National Park, 133
riverbed turtle, 45
riverine habitat, 70
roan, 100
rock bass, 104
rock hyraxes, 6
rollers, 69–70, 102
rondavels (thatched chalets), 65
Roosevelt, Theodore, 9
rosyfaced lovebirds, 100
Rovuma River, 125
Ruaha National Park, 137
Rudolph, Lake (Turkana), 39, 56
Ruwenzori Mountains, 9, 79–89
Ruwenzori National Park, 81–82, 138
Rwanda, parks and reserves of, 136

Sabi Sand game preserve, 111
sable, 100, 123
saddle area, of Kilimanjaro, 6
safari ants, 57
Safari River Lodge, 16
safari trips, practical guide for, 141–44
safety issues: political unrest, xv; transportation, 28, 60, 61,
    65, 114–15
St. Lucia nature preserve, 115–16
salt lick, as gathering place for wildlife, 27
Salt Lick Sanctuary, 15–16, 16, 134
Samburu Game Lodge, 66, 68–69, 135
Samburu National Park, 65–70, 134–35
sanctuaries, wildlife. See parks, summary of
sand dunes, Namib, 106
sand grouse, 17, 46, 102
sandpipers, 39
Sani Pass, 115
Sani Pass Hotel, 114
San people (Kalahari Bushmen), 94, 115
savannah, African. See great plains
Savuti area, 122
Schaller, George, 48
seals, Cape fur, 104, 106
seasonal events, in Serengeti, 47
secretary bird, 35, 44, 49, 69, 119
Selous Game Reserve, 137
Serengeti National Park, 4, 43, 137–38
Serengeti Plain, 7, 43–52. See also Olduvai Gorge
Serengeti Shall Not Die (Grzimek), 63
Seronera Wildlife Lodge, 49, 138
Sesreim Canyon, 105
Shimba Hills Game Reserve, 135
Shire Highlands, 124
sitatunga, 95
siwantherium, 56
Skeleton Coast Park, 103–104, 136
slash-and-burn farming, 25
slave trade, African, 128
snakes, 85, 100
Snows of Kilimanjaro, The (Hemingway), 5
social weavers, 102
soda lakes, 37, 39
soil quality, Serengeti, 45
Solitaire camp, 105
songbirds, 35
Sossuvie camp, 105

South Africa, 9, 109–19, 136–37

Sowa pans, 92

spadefoot toad, 45

species losses, in rainforest areas, 25. *See also* endangerment of wildlife

Speke, Capt. John, 9

spitting cobras, 85

spoonbills, 39

spotted hyena: at Aberdare, 27, 30–32; birds as prey of, 37; vs. brown, 93; and lion kills, 47; at Ngorongoro, 60, 62–63

springbok: Kalahari, 92, 93, 94; Namibia, 102, 103; South Africa, 112, 116, 119

square-lipped rhinoceros, 6, 70, 74–75, *75,* 114

Stanley, Henry M., *7,* 9, 80, 125–28, 130

steenbok, *112*

storks: Lake Bogoria, 37; Lake Manyara, 58; Lake Nakuru, 39; Orange Free State, 113; Ruwenzori, 82; Serengeti, 44, 46

struggle for survival, 29–32

Sultan's palace, Zanzibar, *127*

Sumba Game Preserve, 139

sunbirds, 69–70, 113

surf fishing, Skeleton Coast, 103–104

Swakopmund, Namibia, 104

swales, 45

swarthaak acacias, 101

sycamore figs, 101

Table Mountain, 116

Taita Hills, 6, 15, 17

tamoboti, 102–103

Tana River, 6, 70

Tanganyika, Lake, 7, 9, 35, 128

Tanzania: as best climbing approach to Kilimanjaro, 5; lakes of, 35, 56–58; nesting flamingos in, 39; Olduvai Gorge, 55–56; and overthrow of Idi Amin, 88; parks and reserves of, 137–38; and Serengeti, 43

Tarangire National Park, 138

tawny eagle, 37, 102

Telekei Valley, 32, 134

termite mounds, 82, 85–88, *87*

Thompson's Falls, 26

Thompson's gazelle: Manyara Lake, 56; Ngorongoro, 61; Serengeti, 44, 47, 49, 52

thorny scrub, 17

tick birds, 81

tigers, 76

tilapia fish, 17, 41

timing of safari trips, 142

Tiva River, 17

tommies. *See* Thompson's gazelle

Top Hut, 6, 7

topi, 44, 47, 49, 52

tour groups, advantage of, 65

transfer stations, 27

transportation: arrangements for, 142; availability, 32; cross-Nile, 82; dangers of, 114–15; difficulties of, 60, 61, 65; and isolation of Lake Malawi, 41; in Okavango, 95

Transvaal area, 110–11

trees: in Aberdare, 27; acacia, 17, 44, 45, 99, 105; baobab, 17, 19, 123; candelabra, 38; fever, 45; fig, 95, 101; kokerboom, 99; makalani palms, 102–103; *Moringa ovalifolia,* 103; podocarpus, 79; in South Africa, 112

Treetops Lodge, 26–27

tribes: Bushmen, Kalahari, 94, 115; Chagga, 8, 9; Demara, 101; Herero, 101; Masai, 8, 57, 59; Nilotic, 88; Pokot, 65; Zulu, 113

trophy game animals, historical collection of, 9

Tsavo National Park, 6, 8, 16–23, 135

tsessebe, 100

tundra, alpine, Kilimanjaro, 5

Turkana, Lake, 39, 56

Uganda, 88, 138

Uganda kob, 81

Ugandan ecosystem, 79–89

Ujiji, 128

umbrella acacias, 45, 101

Umolozi game reserve, 114

Upington, Botswana, 93

Upington, South Africa, 117

vaal rhebok, 112

Vaal River, 110

Van der Decken's hornbills, 58

vehicle needs. *See* transportation

vervet monkeys, 17, 37

Victoria, Lake, 7, 81

Victoria Falls National Park, 123, 139

Virunga mountains, 88–89

Visoke, Mount, 88

volcanoes, 3–10, 26, 55–63

vultures: bearded, 56, 112, 115; black, 46; Cape, 100–101; griffin, 51; in Samburu, 69

Waller's gazelle, 66
Walvis Bay, 104
Wanke National Park, 139
warthogs, *117;* Namibia, 100; Okavango, 94; Salt Lick, 15; Samburu, 67; Tsavo, 17
Waterberg Park for Endangered Species, 99, 100–101, 136
waterbuck, 36, 37, 38
waterfalls, 26, 27, 68, 82, *83, 85,* 123
waterfowl: Aberdare, 27, 29; Kalahari, 93; Lake Manyara, 58; Okavango, 95; Rift Valley lakes, 35–41; Ruwenzori, 81, 82, *85;* Samburu, 69–70; Serengeti, 44, 46; South Africa, 118; Tsavo, 17
waterholes, 15, 17, 27, 29, 45, 94
weather and elevation considerations, 142
weaver birds, 69–70, 102, 113
Welwitshia mirabilis plant, 103
West Coast Provincial National Park, 117–18
Western, David, 14
whales, 118
White Nile, 80
White Nile, The (Moorhead), 126–27
white rhinoceros, 6, 70, 74–75, *75,* 114
wild dogs, 47–48, 69, *71,* 102, 114
wildebeest, *125;* Kalahari, 93, 94; Meru, 73; Ngorongoro Crater, 59, 61; Okavango, 95; Serengeti, 43–44, 45, 47, 49, 50–52; South Africa, 111, 112–13, 116, 119; Tsavo, 17; Zambia, 138
wildlife park, definition, 131
Willem Pretorius Game Reserve, 113
Windhoek, Namibia, 99
Wolters, Edmund, 113
World Wildlife Fund, 14, 38, 40

Xaxaba Camp, 95

yellow baboons, 73
yellow-billed storks, 39
Yemen, as source of rhino horn demand, 76

Zaire, parks and reserves of, 138
Zambezi River, 122–24
Zambia, 39, 127–28, 138–39
Zanzibar, 6
zebras, *123, 124;* Kalahari, 93, 94; Meru, 73; Namibia, 102, 103; Ngorongoro, 59, 61; Ruwenzori, 81; Salt Lick Sanctuary, 15; Samburu, 67; Serengeti, 44, 47, 49, *50;* South Africa, 111, 112, 114, 116; Tsavo, 17
Zimbabwe, parks and reserves of, 139
Zululand, 113–16